The Women of Block 12

VOICES FROM A JAIL MINISTRY

LINDA PISCHKE

THE WOMEN OF BLOCK 12

Published by Linda Pischke

© 2011 by Linda L. Pischke

International Standard Book Number: 978-0-9712706-1-9

Cover, interior design and typeset by Dawn Pekel, Arising Design

**QUANTITY DISCOUNTS ARE AVAILABLE TO YOUR ORGANIZATION
FOR GIFTS, FUND-RAISING, OR EDUCATIONAL PURPOSES.**

FOR MORE INFORMATION:

Linda Pischke
P.O. Box 666
Mukwonago, WI 53149
lpischke@lindapischke.com

Pischke
Publications

This book is dedicated to the women
of Block 12 and all women who are confined
to prisons of concrete and steel, prisons of
abusive relationships, prisions of addiction, or
prisons of shame and regret.

—ɯ—

TABLE OF CONTENTS

PREFACE

*W*hy jail ministry? If someone had asked me that question in 2001, I simply would have said, "Because Father Joe called me." Joe was a retired priest and chaplain of the St. Vincent de Paul Jail Ministry in our community. He told me he had been praying for someone to write a jail newsletter and I was the answer to his prayers. Surely the man was confused. Why would God choose someone like me, a lukewarm Lutheran with no prior experience and a lack of sympathy for people who broke the law?

I was familiar with Christ's words, "I was in prison and you visited me" (Matthew 25:36, NLT), but I didn't have the slightest idea what that really meant. Jesus in prison! That's not what I thought of when I watched the evening news. Those people were thieves and murderers. They messed up. They were right where they belonged, and I was pretty sure there weren't any real Christians among them.

For years I had been living on promises to God. "I'll work for you someday—someday when the kids are grown, someday when I don't have a full-time job, someday when I'm not so busy."

But the day never came, and my mailbox was filled with offers for senior discounts. I checked my spiritual resume. It was still blank, and time was running out.

My best friend assured me there was no mistake. God was calling *me*. Since she seemed to be more in tune with the Holy Spirit, I took her word for it and accepted the job. It was an act of obedience without a lot of heart. The newsletter assignment would have to do. I could meet God's requirements for service, and I'd never have to get up close and personal with the inmates.

Long-distance help was not exactly what God had in mind. Like all volunteer jobs, one thing led to the next, and I received a call to Block 12, a housing unit for women awaiting trial.

"Would you consider leading a women's group?" they asked.

Mentoring criminals was not my idea of service for the Lord. On the one hand I was afraid of them; on the other I had the self-righteous idea that I could teach them a thing or two. I began my ministry believing it was my job to take Jesus to the jail and introduce him to the inmates, but he was already there waiting for me.

I found him in the gymnasium on Sunday mornings with Father Joe and in the long, cold hallways when the guard, at my side, professed his faith. Jesus joined us in the classroom where we gathered to sing and pray, and the women assured me he was in their cells when they cried themselves to sleep. Yes, my Jesus was there with the drug addicts and prostitutes waiting for me to visit him, and I discovered he is their Jesus, too.

—m—

The Women Of Block 12 is a journey into a world that, thankfully, most of us will never experience. It is a world of broken childhoods and shattered dreams, a world of chaos and utter despair. It is the story of the more than 200,000 female offenders who occupy beds in America's jails and prisons.

We despise them. We call them names. We define them by their crimes and make them pay for what they have done—over and over again—but we never quite forgive them. Will we continue to hold them hostage when they return to our communities, chained to the past in a cycle of recidivism, or will we help them to heal through the love of Jesus Christ?

Why jail ministry? I was called to tell their story.

PART ONE – Two Worlds. The events in chapters one through eleven tell the intimate and heartwarming story of my encounters with the women of Block 12, an experience that forever changed my view of crime and criminals. During the time of this story, 2001 to 2010, our community built a new jail. It is bigger, safer, and more impersonal. The women were moved several times to new cellblocks called pods. As a result, the location of our classroom changed. For purposes of simplicity and ease of reading, I continued to refer to the location as Block 12. The stories in this section are true, but all names and identifying information have been changed to protect the privacy of those involved.

PART TWO – The Women's Stories. The personal narratives in this section are recorded exactly as told to me. The individual writers chose how and what to reveal about the details of their lives. Occasionally, the language is offensive, but it was not my intention to edit the stories for purposes of writing style or content. Some of the chapters may seem long and tiresome. They are presented "as is" to emphasize the repetition, frustration, and futility of lives driven by mental illness and drug abuse. Many of the authors chose to use their real names, and some have disguised their identity. Not all of the contributors lived in Block 12. Five biographies came by referral from former class members. I believe these stories are a true representation of the non-violent female offenders who live in our nation's prisons and jails.

PART THREE – A Brief Guide To Jail and Prison Ministry. When we can't love ourselves, it sometimes takes another person to show us we are lovable. This, I believe, is the responsibility of the church. We are called to minister to the poor, the sick, the naked, the hungry, and the imprisoned wherever we can find them. The purpose of jail and prison ministry is not to excuse unlawful activity or feel sorry for offenders, but to bring healing to everyone touched by crime through the power of God's love and forgiveness. The suggestions in this section are only a beginning. There are many opportunities to serve.

—⚍—

THANK YOU

*T*he following individuals and organizations, through their generous contributions of financial support and personal time, have made it possible to publish this work for the benefit of prison, jail, and aftercare ministries. Your faith in my ability to finish this project has been inspirational.

Thank you to Kay Styza, Paul Noran, the Swanto family, Karen McQuestion, Carolyn Stoddard, St. Andrew's Lutheran Church, Plowshare Inc., Lynette Wanasek, John Quaal, St. John's Lutheran Church, Gethsemane Lutheran Church, Avalon Square, Diane Hatchell, and Gail Grenier Sweet for their financial support.

My thanks to Lynette Wanasek who insisted I visit the jail for the first time and made sure I stayed on task. Thanks to Susie Mihaljevich and Jill Turcott-Nielsen who listened tirelessly while I shared ideas and read chapters for their approval and who always believed I could do this. Thank you to Kathy Kaufman, Karen McQuestion, and the Chapter One Writing Group for mentoring me. Thank you to Jack and Kathleen Congleton, JoAnne Konkel, Karen McQuestion, Susie Mihaljevich, and Judith Williams for editing and corrections. Thank you, Dawn Pekel for the contribution of your artistic talents and Ellen Kozak for legal advice. Love and thanks to my family for their patience over the last eight years when I said, "Don't bother me, I'm writing."

Special thanks to the women who have generously contributed their personal stories in the hope that others will benefit from their life experiences: Robyn, Pamela, Joy, Barbara, Diane, Tammie, Michelle M., Michelle S., Star, Lynn, Yolanda, Ann, Carol, and Tesa. You have enriched and blessed my life.

—〰—

INTRODUCTION

*M*y father used to say, "Those people are cut from a different cloth," referring to anyone who didn't act or live the way we did. The phrase was his response to news stories covering crimes of passion, drunk driving accidents, even race riots. It was his excuse for religious wars in the Middle East and the unusual lifestyles of hippies and flower children. With words like, "cut from a different cloth," Dad somehow justified a person's actions, giving him the benefit of the doubt and placing some burden of guilt on his or her circumstances. I believe it was a term he used to explain the behaviors of people he didn't understand, and it helped him to make sense of a world that was supposed to be filled with love and kindness.

It was the 1950s. Our family belonged to a group of educated suburbanites who went to church every week and believed Ozzie and Harriet were our neighbors. Crime was something that happened in the city, and people of a "different cloth" rarely crossed our path.

I learned to see myself as better than others and came to define our family and the place we lived as somehow superior. In our neighborhood, people followed the rules—or tried to. Never mind the man who had a heart attack two blocks from home in his girlfriend's bed or the mother who drove the family car into the garage and closed the door with the engine running. And there was the pastor who favored altar boys and the football coach who slept with cheerleaders. Those were the exceptions. We were different. Our cloth was of a finer grade.

While my parents served on church committees, I served myself. They taught me to sit in the front pew. I felt safer in the back. From there I could critique the rest of the congregation and give at a distance—checks in the offering plate, groceries for the food pantry—and never touch anyone who was different. Over the years, the burden of these beliefs weighed heavily on my life, and I turned inward, pulling my finely woven cloth firmly around me to shut out the world and other hurting people.

God knew I needed a large dose of humility, the kind you swallow when you realize you're no better than anyone else, so he called me to ministry at the county jail. There, in a tiny barbershop-turned-classroom, I met the women who would change my life forever.

We gathered on Wednesday nights, a mismatched group of strangers crammed into a room just big enough to seat twelve around a table. There I handed out paper and pencils to women dressed in orange who lived in the ghetto, working-class row-houses, and suburban mansions. There were mothers, daughters, sisters, even grandmothers, and they represented every race, religion, and ethnic group in our community.

Any ideas I had about being different were soon put to rest. The jail was a great equalizer and our classroom a melting pot. In that room, no one really cared which neighborhood you came from or the cut of your cloth.

I came to the jail to be a teacher, but God had other plans. He wanted me to learn. My instructors were women of a different cloth, women who opened their hearts to teach me about life, faith, and the true meaning of friendship. This is their story.

—m—

PART 1
Two Worlds

I sought my soul,
But my soul I could not see.
I sought my God,
But my God eluded me.
I sought my sisters and I found all three.

ANONYMOUS

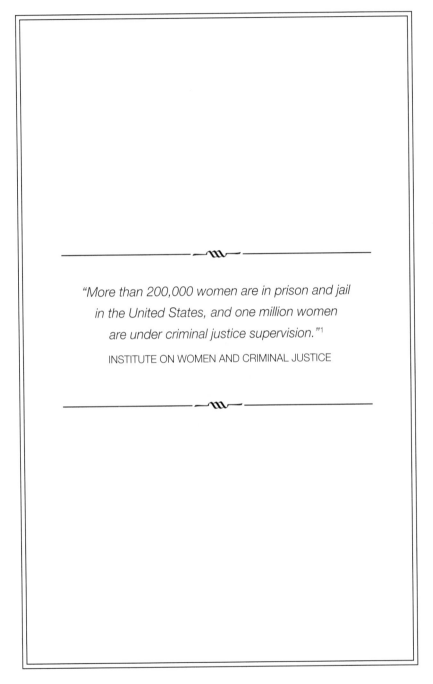

"More than 200,000 women are in prison and jail in the United States, and one million women are under criminal justice supervision."[1]

INSTITUTE ON WOMEN AND CRIMINAL JUSTICE

CHAPTER 1
The Block

—⬩⬩⬩—

When I close my eyes, I see their faces: young and old, brown and white, pretty and plain. The women of Block 12 are always with me, forever woven into the fabric of my life, members in a growing family of those for whom I pray.

Amber is tall and slender, nineteen years old, with the face and body of a super model. She is part African-American, part Native American. "Cherokee," she tells me, and she thinks she's ugly.

Savanah has masses of blonde curls that bush out around her pale blue eyes and rosy pink complexion. She's the all-American girl-next-door who is drinking herself to death.

Nasim is from the Middle East. Her cellmates tell me she speaks no English and is being held for her alien status. They wrap their arms around her when she cries and comfort her with soothing voices. As a sign of acceptance, they have braided her thick brown hair into cornrows. She is one of them for now. Nasim does not know what will happen to her American-born children when she is extradited to her homeland.

Tina's sweet pixie face is pale and drawn. " I just finished chemo," she says, self-consciously running her fingers through short wisps of new brown hair. "I have lymphoma."

Shandra is tiny with smooth chocolate skin. Her cornrows are tipped in gray. She lowers her head and peers at me over clear, acrylic half-readers (a gift from the jail ministry).

"I like your purple specs," she says. We laugh together and share the names of our grandchildren. She will not see hers again until they are grown.

Block 12 houses an ever-changing population of drug addicts, alcoholics, prostitutes, and the mentally ill. A temporary residence in our local jail, the women who live there are non-violent offenders incarcerated for driving under the influence, possession of controlled substances, domestic violence, and petty theft or fraud. While some call Block 12 "home" for a few weeks or months, others may stay a year or more. These inmates are in a state of waiting: waiting for trial, waiting to be moved to another jail or prison, waiting to go home.

The block holds fourteen females, the term used by jail personnel to identify the inmates. Officers of both genders shout a variety of messages through metallic-sounding intercoms.

"There will be ten females attending your group this evening."

"Visitors may leave the classroom. Females, please be seated and wait for transport."

"Females will be checked for contraband before returning to the block."

"Females are not allowed to have pencils with erasers on them."

The women refer to themselves in a more personal way using the terms "women" or "ladies" in their conversation.

I have been told it is an honor to live in Block 12, a privilege earned by good behavior. Since there is limited space, a person who has achieved Block 12 status may have to wait weeks or months to be transferred from another block, and her turn may not come until after she is released or moved to another facility. Once on the block, an inmate may attend general education classes, Bible study, one Alcoholics Anonymous (AA) meeting per week, Alcohol and Other Drug Addictions (AODA) education groups, and worship services. Twice a week she can go for a walk in the gym, if the guards choose to take her. Outside exercise is available only to male inmates. Other amenities (donated by the jail ministry) include luxuries such as a coffee pot to provide hot water for mixing cocoa or cooking ramen noodles (items available from the canteen), a television, movies, a DVD player, board games, puzzles and soft-cover books.

Over the past eight years, I have met hundreds of Block 12 women, ten or twelve at a time. We gather on Wednesday evenings in the barbershop-turned-classroom on the main floor of the county jail. We read books, write poetry, share our lives, and worship together. Week after week, the women file into the tiny concrete room dressed in orange two-piece scrubs with peach undershirts, peach socks, and tan plastic sandals. I wonder if peach is a fashion statement, or the result of washing white underclothes with orange suits. The room holds twelve chairs and when everyone is seated around the table, our shoulders are touching.

The women are bathed and their hair is clean, but a faint smell of locker-room mustiness enters the classroom with them. Stripped of their jewelry, hair spray, body lotions, and perfumes, there is a false aura of innocence about them. No secrets here. No hiding behind Maybelline lips and Cover Girl eyes. Each face is revealed, scrubbed clear down to the blemishes, exposed like their lives to public view. I search their faces seeking familiarity and wonder if I have shopped alongside them at the mall.

As teacher and mentor to these women, I have come to see their beauty and love every one of them. I am invariably surprised by their similarities to the "normal" people around me. I am touched by their kindness and sensitivity. Most of all, I am ashamed that I thought it would be any other way.

I look into their eyes and see all women—my sisters, my neighbors, and my friends. Robyn's eyes are sad, the big round eyes of a beautiful child in the face of a thirty-something woman. She wears navy blue scrubs, the uniform of a trustee. This honor is extended to a select few in the block. Robyn is allowed to work off some of her sentence, one hour at a time, cleaning floors late into the night. Her straight brown hair hangs below her shoulders, and she looks very tired. Robyn is working her Twelve-Step Program with an Alcoholics Anonymous sponsor.

"I've been an addict since I was fourteen," she admits. " I've done this before, but I avoided some of the hard parts. I never wanted to do a fearless moral inventory where I told my sponsor everything about my life. This time I'm going to make it."

Robyn writes about the block:

> We all live in an L-shaped room with fourteen metal bunks stacked two deep. At the back of the room there is a glass textured wall and door that opens into the two-stall, two-shower bathroom. Each stall has a metal toilet (no toilet seat) and attached metal sink with two buttons mounted on the side of the basin to push for hot or cold water. The water comes out of a drinking-fountain-type spout at

the top of the sink. One hand must be used to hold the water button down and the other can reach the water. Having hot and cold water at the same time and washing two hands at a time are a thing of the past once you are incarcerated. The hot water is controlled by the guards somewhere outside of the block and is typically turned on only during shower time (from 9:00 pm until all fourteen women are done, or until 10:30 pm—whichever comes first).

There are no secrets in Block 12. Fourteen women are crowded together, and the stress is high. There are so many different personalities, and you're in a setting where you cannot be alone. In addition, there is the strain of being incarcerated. The things that the average person holds the most private are out there for public ridicule and scorn.

The guards come to the door and yell, "Who's going to AODA class?"

The nurse yells your name and has any and all conversations about your personal conditions and medications in front of the others. Once a week, a large bucket with community underwear is pushed into the block, and fourteen women compete for the cleanest pairs, shouting things like, "Who needs a 34C bra?"

I feel really sad that the people who make the decisions of who is held there and for how long don't know the conditions. Sometimes, I get on my bunk and pull my semi-clean sheets and musty wool blanket over my head and just cry.

—␣—

―∽―

"The United States has less than 5 percent of the world's population but leads the world in producing prisoners— 2.3 million or one-fourth of the world's prison population."[2]

INTERNATIONAL CENTER FOR PRISON STUDIES

―∽―

CHAPTER 2

Papa Joe

—⟫⟫—

*I*t was Father Joe who called me, not by phone, mind you, but called me in the Biblical sense, something I had never experienced before. He called me to jail ministry, the most unlikely match of volunteer to community need that you could imagine. Until then, I was a lukewarm Christian who occupied a pew at the back of the church once or twice a month and whose benevolence resume was limited to a three-year stretch of teaching fifth-grade Sunday school.

That's not exactly the way I had been raised, you understand. My parents were front-row Lutherans who never missed a Sunday and spent their lives in faithful service to the church. Their example rubbed off on my older sister. She sang in the choir, led Bible studies, and served wherever she was needed. Not me. I kept my distance. My faith, though firmly grounded, was on the inside, held tightly in the privacy of my heart, and I knew it was not enough.

I worked full-time as a nursing-home social worker. I got paid for that and really didn't think it counted as service for the Lord, so I promised myself that, some day, when I had time to do something more than make a few casseroles for shut-ins and empty my coin purse into red buckets at Christmas, I would volunteer. I would make a difference, somehow. But I had no idea what that something would be or how I would go about doing it.

Joe was the chaplain of our county jail, an ex-priest addressed by many as Father but known to his flock as Papa Joe. I met him at my day job in the last year of his ministry. He came highly recommended as a speaker for our senior volunteer group at the nursing home. We were looking for a community project where we could serve people in need, and Joe's parishioners had many needs. I contacted him with the help of a mutual friend, and he accepted our invitation to speak.

A senior himself, Joe fit right in with the nursing home residents. He was confined to a wheelchair and required the assistance of a companion to drive him to and from the jail. Despite his age and failing health, he was a spiritual giant with a passion for the incarcerated. Joe conducted Sunday services and made daily visits to the inmates. He wrote letters on behalf of those who were scheduled to appear in court and helped them find shelter when they were released.

"Most of the time, I just listen," he said, "and I pray with them all—Christians, Muslims, Jews—we have to be sensitive to other religions."

Joe told us that his passion for prison ministry began with a life-changing experience when he was a young priest.

"I was driving downtown," he said, "and I looked out of my window. There to my left was a bum, lying on the ground, sick and unconscious. He was unshaved and poorly dressed. Liquid was flowing from his mouth onto the sidewalk.

"My first impulse was to take care of the man, an example I learned from my dad, but then I thought about my nice clean suit and the fact that I would be late for my doctor's appointment. I figured someone would be along soon to take care of the old timer, so I didn't stop. Oh, did God let me have it! I felt terrible, terrible. By then I was several blocks away.

"The guilt I experienced affected my entire life. From then on I didn't want God pointing a finger at me. I realized it was my job to care for somebody who was in a mess, even if they made the mess themselves.

"Over the years," Joe continued, "I came to have a fascination with folks who ruined their lives in a criminal way. When you see those folks up there at the jail, you might say, 'They made their own mess; let them lie in it,' but, no, that's your brother."

The seniors and I were drawn to his stories of the men and women who called the jail home. Joe personally agonized over the loneliness and despair of his congregation, their shattered lives, and repeated failures. He longed to fill their hunger for the Word, to set them straight with their God. That day, at the nursing home, he spoke to our group in slow, deliberate phrases often closing his eyes and tilting his head back as if to capture a vision.

"The hardest part of my work is the sheer tragedy of it," he said. "Those men and women have lost their jobs. They have to leave their families. They live in disgrace. I can never get used to it. And yet, some of them surprise me. They decide to turn their lives around, to take a path that is worthwhile. I have no numbers, but many have told me that it was a turning point in their lives when we worked together on their souls."

GRANNIES AND JAILBIRDS

As Joe talked, I saw a picture forming: seniors and inmates. One group was elderly, the other youthful. Both were lonely, both institutionalized. In my mind, it was a perfect union. Our nursing-home residents would become partners in Joe's jail ministry.

The seniors made cards and baked cookies. My co-workers made fun of me.

"You could call it the Grannies and Jailbirds Project," one suggested.

Others openly expressed their anger. "Why are you giving gifts to inmates?" they asked. "Those people deserve punishment, not presents."

I didn't have an answer. My personal knowledge of criminals was limited to watching media coverage of men and women standing before a judge in handcuffs. How could I defend a group of people I didn't understand? I decided to rely on the compassion of Father Joe. If he felt our project helped the men and women at the jail, it was good enough for me.

The program was a success. Father Joe became a familiar visitor to the nursing home and a friend to the seniors. We sent holiday treats to the jail. The inmates sent us posters, drawings, and notes of thanks.

For me, it became personal. I read the thank-you letters and studied the drawings over and over again. Jenna, Carlos, Tom, Kyeisha, Mary R. The men and women of our county jail now had names, a fact I was not prepared to accept. I knew it would be easier to put it all aside, to think of them as faceless criminals. I wanted to believe they were not my responsibility, but the whole thing really bothered me.

I'm doing my part. I argued with God. *We make cookies and send holiday gift bags. I'm really working hard at this, and I'm spending a lot more time volunteering than I used to. Look at all these good works! The seniors are busy and feeling useful. The inmates are getting something out of this, too.*

It was then he reminded me that I should understand. Of course, I should. My job was a daily witness to the loneliness of men and women in their eighties and nineties who supposedly had outlived their usefulness to society. Like the inmates, they were isolated and invisible behind institutional walls.

FINDING OUT WHAT GOD WANTS

Father Joe invited our seniors to the jail, a one-time visit and tour of the facilities. I was sick the day of the field trip and didn't get to go. A few weeks later, my job was eliminated, and I joined the unemployed.

Months passed. From time to time, the thought would occur to me, *Father Joe invited you to the jail and you never went. Just go see it.*

I ignored the urge. I no longer wanted to be involved, but the thought kept coming back and I couldn't put it to rest. After a long period of unemployment, I casually mentioned the concern to my best friend, Lynette.

"I keep thinking about visiting the jail, but I don't really want to go."

By then, she was getting tired of the " poor me, I'm out of a job" conversation, so she said, "Well, girl, you'd better go find out what God wants from you!"

"That sounds like an order!" I replied.

"I guess it is," she said laughing, "but I don't really know why I said it."

I knew Lynette was right and I knew she would hold me accountable. I took the challenge and phoned Father Joe. He was delighted to hear my voice and invited me to services the following Sunday.

A DIFFERENT KIND OF SANCTUARY

Christ calls us to visit him in the humblest of places: among the poor, the sick, the elderly, and the imprisoned. That Sunday morning, I found him at the county jail. There in the gray-tiled gymnasium with its high ceilings and glaring lights, inmates gathered to worship. Twenty men entered, single file, their orange-glow suits brilliant against the white walls. Each carried a molded plastic chair and placed it in a semi-circle facing the elderly chaplain.

Amid sounds of clanging doors and echoing voices, the men crowded around Father Joe's wheelchair, smiling, shaking his hand, eager for words of encouragement. I walked up to the group hoping my anxiety didn't show.

"Welcome, friend," Joe greeted me. "Guys, this is Linda. She's from the nursing home, the one responsible for all those wonderful gift bags you got Easter Sunday."

One by one the inmates walked up to me and introduced themselves. Young pimply-faced boys and balding men extended their hands in greeting. The shy ones stared at the floor when they mumbled their names. Others eagerly grasped my hand in both of theirs. "Thank you for coming today. God bless you!"

Their greetings were unhurried, and I experienced an unexpected sense of calm. Here in this unlikely place of worship, I felt more welcomed than in my own church where, year after year, I sat in the back pew with people I could not call by name. Like them, I "shared the peace" with quick handshakes, frozen smiles, and an urgency to move on. In this sanctuary, as the men paused to welcome me, they were sincere. Joe was their mentor, their pastor, and their friend. He demonstrated the love of Christ to this assembly of outcasts, and they in turn extended it to me.

Joe's face crinkled into a grimace, then brightened, his white eyebrows lifting as if a thought had just come to him. His eyes met mine. "We've been looking for someone to write a newsletter for the jail."

"I can do that!" I said without thinking. The words tumbled from my mouth as if my friend had just elbowed me in the ribs and whispered, "Raise your hand for this one!"

And before I could take it all back, Joe lifted his hands heavenward and said, "Praise the Lord! Gentlemen, our prayers have been answered."

—ᴍ—

It was time to begin. I was asked to pass out missals. The men took their seats. One offered me his chair, then sat on the floor. It was a simple service without the benefit of organ music or the beauty of sunlight filtering through stained-glass windows. There was no altar or cross. And yet I sensed God's presence, as I'd never personally experienced it in church. This was the body of Christ in prison. This was holy ground.

The concrete walls echoed every cough and the shuffling of feet. One man whispered the sermon to another in Spanish, and the congregation strained to hear the voice of the elderly chaplain they affectionately called Papa Joe.

And so, I understood the call. My friend was right. God had been urging me all along. I just wasn't listening. But as soon as I walked into that gymnasium, I heard him loud and clear. I am a writer. The jail needed a newsletter. Okay. I got the message!

THE BAR NONE

A week later, the Newsletter Executive Committee was formed. Joe, the jail captain, and I met exactly one time over lunch in Father Joe's kitchen. We agreed upon a format: body, mind, and spirit. The newsletter would include health and fitness, educational articles, a faith-based page, and space for inmate submissions. Beyond that, the rest was up to me.

There were a few problems. We had no money to buy paper or print the needed 350 copies. At the meeting, I forgot to mention that I had never written a newsletter or even worked on one. Nor did I admit that my word-processing skills fell into the remedial-learning category. I figured a promise is a promise, and if God and the jail wanted a newsletter…well, prayer is a powerful thing.

Within weeks our prayers were answered. A friend began to tutor me in the needed computer skills, and a local congregation with a full-scale print shop stepped forward and offered us anything we needed, including free use of their graphic artist and unlimited printing services. We started with a flyer announcing our intentions and asked the inmates to name the paper. In the fall of 2001, The Bar None newsletter was born.

One year into the writing of the newsletter, Father Joe retired. The new chaplain called me. Could I please help her out with the Wednesday night Bible study for the women of Block Twelve?

Me? You want me to conduct a Bible study, Lord? Not on your life!

But…I could teach a journaling class.

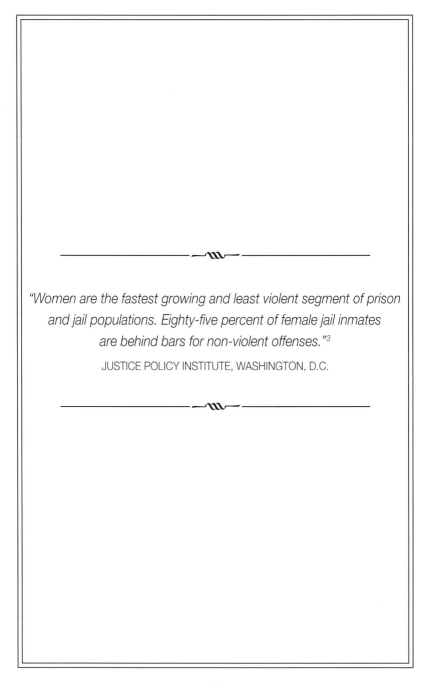

"Women are the fastest growing and least violent segment of prison and jail populations. Eighty-five percent of female jail inmates are behind bars for non-violent offenses."[3]

JUSTICE POLICY INSTITUTE, WASHINGTON, D.C.

CHAPTER 3
Standing in the Gap

—⚏—

C haplain Martha's request for help with the Bible study took me by
surprise. Until then, I managed to keep my distance. I coordinated
the publication of the Bar None newsletter and attended monthly
jail ministry meetings. I was quite content with this arrangement, believing I
was doing what God had asked. It fit well into my schedule, and despite the
positive experience of that earlier Sunday service with Father Joe, I was not
planning to get up close and personal with the prisoners.

A journaling class! What was I thinking? I don't even keep a journal.
Once again, words had just popped out of my mouth, and I volunteered to do
something for which I had no personal experience.

Questions circled in my head. Who were these women in the Wednesday
night Bible study? How do I talk to them? Are they dangerous? Can they read
and write? What if I don't like them? What if they don't like me?

Perhaps that last thought scared me the most. What if these women
found out what I was really like—an insecure, self-help junkie addicted to
philosophers like Oprah and Dr. Phil? I talked too much and craved the acceptance of...well, everyone. I held grudges, let people walk all over me, and
possessed talents I didn't share. I was clueless about my purpose in life. God
needed a holy person to minister under these circumstances, not someone
who was struggling with her own spirituality.

There was also the little matter of my personal biases, attitudes cultivated
over the course of a lifetime in the company of family and friends, a collection
of opinions admittedly influenced by the six o'clock news. I could sum it up in
just one sentence.

"Don't break the law, and you won't go to jail."

I believed the barriers between "us and them," the free and the incarcerated, were created by their own poor choices, and I was convinced those women in the Bible study class were exactly where they belonged.

THE BARBERSHOP

Chaplain Martha and I walked through a metal detector and handed our identification cards to the officer on duty. He searched our bags.

"Bibles, pencils, notebooks with no wires. Okay, ladies," he said, holding the door to let us pass. "You may go into the barbershop. The females will join you shortly."

A wall of black windows stared at us as we walked by the control room. We moved about ten feet and came to a second door. I jumped as the first door slammed shut. Then a buzzer sounded to signal that the next lock was open, and Martha pushed against the heavy door.

Buzz. Bang. Buzz. Bang.

Two more doors locked behind us as we moved through the short corridors of steel and wire-meshed glass. We entered the barbershop, a ten by twelve room with a center table and ten chairs. Three sides of the room were gray concrete block. The fourth had a view of the outer hallway. I chose a seat facing the window.

"Our attendance has been poor." Martha said. "Of the fourteen women who live in Block 12, only three or four come to this group. Some of them come because there's nothing else to do on Wednesday nights. The group is always changing. The women are in transition, waiting for trial. It's very difficult to hold classes. You might see an inmate for several weeks or only one time. On occasion, the whole group is different."

Voices in the hallway interrupted her. Through the glass door, we could see the women walking toward us. Their oversized orange scrub-suits hung in shapeless folds from their shoulders and hips. The officer who escorted them was neatly dressed in a form-fitting black uniform.

Buzz. Bang. Buzz.

They walked through the outer corridor, then entered the room single file and found seats around the table. The guard left and the door slammed shut, locking us in.

"Good evening and welcome," Martha said. "I'm Chaplain Martha, and I'd like you to meet Linda. She's from our ministry and the editor of the *Bar None* newsletter. I know some of you have been here before, but please introduce yourselves. We'll start with Christy."

"Christy," echoed the first, as she glanced in my direction then looked down in her lap.

"Julie."

"Carmen."

"Robyn."

"Passion."

Their voices were flat and barely audible.

Martha continued. "For the past eight months we've been doing a Bible study together, but I thought you might like a change. Linda has offered to teach a journaling class during this time on Wednesday evenings."

No response. I searched their faces for some sign of interest. Carmen twisted a strand of her long brown hair between her fingers. Julie rocked back and forth, her arms folded tightly across her chest. Passion stretched and yawned.

This will be fun, I thought.

"Let's begin with a word of prayer," Martha continued.

Prayer is good, I said to myself and God. *I could use some of that right now.*

Heads bowed in obedience. While Martha prayed, I wondered what I could possibly offer this sullen group of women.

Did you really want me to do this, God? I prayed, looking for a way out. *Or were you just kidding? Let's go over this one more time, and maybe we can negotiate some other kind of service, like singing in the choir. You're asking me to mix with convicts and sit among sinners? You want me to enter a foreign country, and I don't even speak the language? Maybe I misunderstood and you weren't calling me after all.*

Martha's prayer ended. "Amens" were whispered around the table.

I had the floor. I looked at their faces and smiled. No one smiled back. I wanted to turn and run, but I was locked in. We were all locked in. My instincts told me this was probably God's answer. He was saying, "Go, girl. You can do this!"

So I took a step forward and crossed into unknown territory.

TRUTH OR LIE?

"I want to welcome all of you and thank Chaplain Martha for inviting me. When she asked me to help with this group, I thought you might like to try a few weeks of creative writing."

"What if you don't know how to write?" Carmen asked.

"Not a problem. We'll learn together. But first we're going to have some fun."

I passed out paper and pencils. Passion immediately began to fold her paper into a pleated fan. Christy started to draw.

"This is a get-to-know-you exercise." I continued. "In this class, you do not have to participate. You may just observe if you wish. I will give you five minutes to write down five things about yourself, such as where you were born or how old you are. Tell us any information you want to share. But there's a catch. One of the statements you write must be a lie."

Two of the women looked up at me.

"You mean we're supposed to tell a lie?" Passion asked. "I thought you ain't supposed to lie."

"Remember, this is just in fun, and when everyone is done, we're going to take turns guessing which statements are true and which are false."

The women stared at me in disbelief, then one by one started to write. Passion pushed aside her fan and asked for another sheet of paper. Martha and I worked on our own lists while they wrote in silence.

"Okay," I said. "Time's up. Who wants to read first?"

"I'll start." Christy cleared her throat. "I'm 24 years old. I was born in Texas. I have three children. I got divorced this year, and I live with my boyfriend."

We started guessing.

"You weren't born in Texas," said Carmen.

"Yes, I was."

"You ain't got no three children."

"I have two boys and a girl."

32

"Are you really 24 years old?" asked Julie.

"No, I'm 19. That was the lie."

"I'll go next," said Julie before anyone else could speak up. "I'm 26 years old. I live with my boyfriend. I speak five languages, I'm going to college, and I have two children."

"It's a lie that you speak five languages," shouted Passion.

"Yeah, you don't speak no five languages," said Carmen, slapping her hand on the table in front of her.

"Actually, I do. English, German, French, Spanish, and Polish."

The room was dead quiet. We all stared at Julie open-mouthed and speechless, just long enough to ask ourselves, *Then what's she doing here? What's a beautiful and well-educated woman doing at the county jail?*

But questions like that were intrusive and unspeakable, so the silence ended and everyone started guessing, at once.

"You're not 26 years old."

"You don't go to college."

"You don't have two children."

"That's it," said Julie. "I have no children, yet."

Passion was next. "Let's see," she said guarding her list like a winning hand of cards. "Uh, I was born in Milwaukee. I have four brothers and three sisters, my father is a minister, I'm not married, and I graduated from high school this year."

"I know your father's a minister." Robyn said. "You told me that when I first met you."

"Were you born in Milwaukee?" Christy asked.

"Yep."

"Are you married?"

"Nope."

"You don't have eight kids in your family," I guessed.

"Yes, we do! Four girls and four boys."

"Well, the only thing left is high school. You must've lied about graduatin,'" said Christy.

"No again," Passion said smiling. "Got you guys! They're all true.

The room exploded into laughter.

That was it! Laughter. Laughter was the universal language, the common denominator between my world and theirs. And even though it lasted only for a moment, I knew we had connected.

CROWD CONTROL

Keeping the connection. That was the challenge. In the weeks to come, I began to understand Chaplain Martha's frustration with the Bible study. Attendance was the biggest obstacle to conducting a group at the county jail. Life there was temporary and unpredictable. Block 12 was a place of transition, a mere pit stop between arrests and court dates, sentencing and final decisions. The women were moved without notice from block to block, city to suburb, maximum to minimum, jail to prison, wherever the system found it necessary to put them.

Interest in the journaling group reflected this uncertainty. If a woman chose to attend, she did so out of curiosity or the desire to escape the intense atmosphere of the block for an hour or two. She might come one time, a few weeks, or a couple of months, and then she was gone.

Some evenings the room was filled with new inmates, and I had to start class all over again. Then, just when I thought I would never see another familiar face, someone would recycle through the system for a violation of probation or parole.

I soon realized that my original plan was unrealistic. A series of writing lessons that flowed smoothly from one week to the next was not practical for a class at the jail. In fact, it was a miserable failure. The block provided no privacy for the women's journals (a barrier to self-expression), and while some of them could write quite well, it was not their primary interest or method of communication. The women were easily bored and lacked the motivation to complete assignments. They were noisy and sometimes took control of the class. I prayed for direction and hoped things would settle down.

One month into the program, Chaplain Martha introduced another ministry member to help with crowd control. Jean was seventy-something with just the right qualifications: retired nurse, mother of five, grandmother of eight. She was a tiny woman with a soft voice and New York accent. Nothing the inmates did shocked or surprised her; after all, she had ushered five grown women safely through the perils of childhood. Jean had a calming effect on the group. God had sent his best.

The women's group was a learn-as-you-go project. Jean opened each class with a prayer or short meditation. We practiced deep breathing and relaxation techniques, tried art therapy and short writing exercises. Jean and I learned each class had to be self-contained, no assignments, nothing left over for the following week. We learned the importance of creating a routine, of letting the women talk until they had nothing left to say. Most of all, we learned the importance of just showing up. And when the women discovered the two of us were there to stay, it settled them.

Our group began to grow, and the little barbershop was soon filled to capacity. No other room was available for the expanding numbers, and we found it necessary to limit attendance to ten inmates. The women worked it out among themselves. A few went to recreation, a weekly privilege that competed for the same time slot. Others took turns and stayed in the block, sending their excuses along the verbal pipeline.

"Reba says to tell you that her lawyer's coming tonight, so she couldn't be here."

"Passion went to court today. She's feelin' poorly. Said to tell you she'll be here next time."

Occasionally, a folded scrap of paper was discreetly placed in front of me.

Dear Linda,
I'm sorry I couldn't come tonight. It's too far to walk from the block to the barbershop because the stitches from my C-section are still hurting. But I'll be there next week, and I promise to bring pictures of the baby. I named him Jamal. Ella

At the end of every evening, our group joined hands to say The Lord's Prayer. One night, after a hearty chorus of "amens," one of the women looked up at me. "I pray for people," she said. "Sometimes I pray for the women in the block, and the next day they get to go home."

"That's called intercessory prayer," I told her. "It's a wonderful gift that you give to others."

"It's called 'standing in the gap,'" said Carmen. "It's when you stand between that person and God and pray for them."

After prayers, Jean and I offered hugs. The women waited in line, and when their turn came, they clung to us like small children not wanting their mothers to leave. With their embraces came whispered confessions, desperate attempts to connect and tell us the deepest of their secrets.

I will never forget Sandi, a young woman who wrapped her arms around me and whispered in my ear, "Last year my two-month-old baby died in a fire. His name was Robbie." Then she laid her head on my shoulder and sobbed until her tears soaked through my jacket. And for the first time, I found myself standing in the gap.

—m—

"The number of women incarcerated in prisons and jails in the United States is approximately ten times more than the number of women incarcerated in Western European countries even though Western Europe's combined female population is about the same size as that of the U.S."[4]

AMNESTY INTERNATIONAL

CHAPTER 4
The Search

—ɯ—

Jean and I entered the jail through the main lobby. The women walked a hallway from the depths of the institution. We wore street clothes. They wore orange. We were free to go at the end of class. They were not. And there the differences that separated us ended. It didn't matter where you lived or what kind of clothes you wore; there were only two kinds of people inside the jail, those who made the rules and those who were expected to obey them. It didn't take long to find out which group I belonged to and the realization stuck in my throat like a dry piece of bread.

Losing my freedom for a couple of hours every week became an exercise in obedience. Everything I wanted to do for the women was at the discretion of the captain. The newsletter was read before publication. Guest speakers went through a background check and turned in an outline of their topic. My program plans were reviewed and usually, but not always, approved. And sometimes, if I had been very good, I could bring a treat for the women. The jail was about rules, and the rules applied to everyone. They protected everyone. They were necessary. They were absolute. Our ministry was there by invitation, and it was clearly understood the welcome mat could be withdrawn at a moment's notice. It was not a democracy but a game of "Captain, May I" and I learned to play it well.

A MATTER OF DIGNITY

When the captain told me I could not give the women pencils, I wanted to ask, "Why?" Instead, I choked back the question, knowing it was not my right, and waited in silence on the other end of the phone, hoping the pause would bring forth an explanation. She didn't offer one. She didn't have to. The rule was enough, and I knew her reason, whatever its source, was just and fair. (I later learned the men had discovered a way to start fires with the metal eraser tips).

So I asked her, "What can I give them?"

"Golf pencils, " she told me.

"What are those?"

"Pew pencils. The kind they use in church."

Pew pencils! I wanted to scream. *Those stubby little yellow things! You've got to be kidding.* But the conversation was over. There would be no discussion. I thanked her and hung up the phone.

The thought of pew pencils angered me and brought to mind an experience I had in the fourth grade. The class was given a test in which you marked your answers by filling in a small space between two lines. The teacher handed out dark green pencils with soft lead points. The opposite ends had no erasers. One student raised his hand.

"How come these pencils don't have any erasers?" he asked.

"So you can't change your answers," the teacher replied.

"So we can't cheat," I said under my breath.

The humiliation of that memory, though forty years past, washed over me and settled in the pit of my stomach. In my mind, giving a woman inmate a pencil without an eraser was a dignity issue. It said I didn't trust her; I expected her to cheat. It took away her freedom to write and erase, to make a decision, or change her mind. I could not give the women pew pencils.

Pride got the best of me. Following the discussion with the captain, I shopped for the prettiest pencils I could find, sawed the ends off and replaced them with colorful eraser caps. They passed inspection and the women loved them. I did not fit easily into the role of submission.

UNWELCOME GUESTS

On Wednesday nights, Jean and I were no different than the women who lived at the county jail, powerless and dependent on the mercy of the guards who found numerous and not-so-subtle ways to keep us in our place. Week after week, we would arrive at the visitor window, pick up the phone, and speak our names and the reason for our visit to an unseen face behind the wall of black glass.

"Jean and Linda from St. Vincent de Paul Jail Ministry. We're here for the women's group."

"Sorry, ma'am, I have no information about that. Who did you say you are?"

And so it went, more questions, delayed responses, and sometimes, long periods of waiting. When the door finally buzzed open and an officer arrived to escort us to the barbershop, he rarely gave eye contact or said "hello." It was clear we were in the way.

As the months passed, we experienced frequent reminders to keep us in our place. Indifference and rudeness were the most common methods, until one particular night when Jean and I were forced to witness a search.

The women formed a line against the wall. No talking, no touching. Class was over, and it was time for transport back to Block 12. Their identical orange scrubs, worn by hundreds of other inmates, hung in folds from their shoulders and waists giving them the appearance of street children in over-sized hand-me-downs. Each woman hugged her notebook and pencil as if they were cherished possessions. This weekly gift from our ministry was tangible proof that someone cared.

Jean and I stood in the hallway with them. It had never happened that way before. We weren't supposed to be outside the barbershop together. On any other Wednesday evening, the protocol kept us separate. One of the women would press the button to announce the end of group, and a voice would boom over the loud speaker.

"Teachers will leave the classroom first. Females wait for escort!"

At the buzzer's sound, we would tug at the heavy door to let ourselves out while the women shouted their last goodbyes. From there we were escorted to the outer part of the jail while the inmates waited for inspection.

That night was different. A female correctional officer opened the door and asked us *all* to step out. The women stopped talking. The air around us seemed to vibrate with tension. Jean turned to me and shrugged as if to say, "What do we do?"

I stared at the officer, seeking her guidance. She refused to look my way and pulled a pair of latex gloves out of her pocket. I glanced at the women and they looked down at their feet, embarrassed by our presence. Everyone knew we were about to witness a search. None of us dared to speak or question our circumstances. One did not question anything at the jail.

Jean and I stood with our backs against the closed door of the classroom trapped in the narrow hallway by the correctional officer (CO) and her charges. I wondered who she was but couldn't read the print on her name tag. Earlier that evening, the women whispered cautions about a CO.

"Don't give us bookmarks or anything extra tonight," Marie mumbled. "Officer S. is on. She'll take them away. She's mean to us. Likes to humiliate people."

"Be careful what you say in this room," Gail said. "They can hear us. You'll get in trouble."

"Yeah, we're not supposed to say anything about the staff," warned another woman.

"I don't care." Marie said a little louder. "She's got it in for all of us. She has family problems and she treats us like sh*t!

The women muffled their giggles.

"I feel kinda bad for her," Gail added. "It's a tough spot to be in, but it's not our fault."

Jean looked at me and raised an eyebrow. I could read her mind. *This must be the CO they were talking about. Had she listened in on our earlier conversation?*

The officer put on the gloves and asked Marie to step forward. She was first in line. Marie handed her notebook and pencil over for inspection and stepped out of her plastic sandals. The officer flipped through the pages of the notebook, turning it upside down to free hidden items. When none appeared, she gave it back and instructed Marie to pass the notebook and her pencil to Kathy who stood next to her.

"Turn around, arms out to your sides," she ordered.

Marie turned.

"NO! Take a step forward, I don't want my back to the wall," demanded the officer. Two of the women looked in our direction.

Marie moved forward and held her arms parallel to the floor. The officer raked her fingers through Marie's shoulder-length hair, fanning it away from her head and letting it fall back in place. Her hands moved around the neck of her orange shirt and proceeded across her shoulders, out to her fingertips, and back toward her body on the underside of her sleeves, down her torso, across the back, and forward under her breasts. She then lifted her shirt a couple of inches and stretched the elastic waistband of her pants enough to loosen any concealed objects. With the waistband back in place she moved her hands down the both sides of Marie's legs from hip to ankle and crotch to socks. Her shoes were also searched.

"Okay, next," the officer said.

Marie took her supplies from Kathy and moved one space forward in line. Kathy handed her notebook to the CO, and the process was repeated nine more times.

At one point, Jean attempted to ease the tension by making small talk with the woman who stood closest to us.

"No talking in line!" shouted the CO, addressing the inmate and ignoring our presence.

The remaining moments were spent in silence except for the soft patting sound of the officer's hands against the women's bodies. The walls closed in around me. I tried not to watch their humiliation. Like the women, Jean and I found no other place to look except down.

I could have reported Officer S. for breaking the rules and allowing us to be in the hallway with the inmates, but I probably would have been told to mind my own business. At worst, she might have received a slap on the hand and then gone back to doing things "by the book." My anger toward her was a waste of time. She knew the women loved the Wednesday evening program and while she couldn't prevent them from going, she could shame them and turn the experience sour.

THE JUDGMENT GAME

I wanted to believe I was different from Officer S., that I could never be that cruel or demeaning to another human being, but it really wasn't true. My cruelty was on the inside, in my heart. There I played the "judgment game," a hurtful practice in which I measured others by the yardstick of my own self-worth. I learned it in the protected culture of my childhood where good and evil were clearly defined and only bad people went to jail. I perfected the game with a lifetime of repetitions. It was easy to play and I'd catch myself practicing whenever I was in the presence of others, on the job, in public, at church. I'd search for comparisons, younger, older, fatter, thinner, smarter, or wealthier. The options were endless and someone always came up the loser. Over the years my beliefs became words and my words became actions, and I wasn't even aware that my life, as a Christian, was a lie—until I came to the county jail.

The "search" was a gift. I was meant to see it, to share in the humiliation and pain. God knew the experience would challenge me and make the game harder to play. I was called, not to change the system, but to change myself. Inside that concrete institution, stripped of my freedom and individuality, I was just like everyone else and only one step away from their circumstances.

Lucky for me, I had learned to sin in socially acceptable ways: gossip, greed, judgment, jealousy, food addictions—the list goes on. And if any of those sins were against the law, I would have been bunking in Block 12.

—〜—

"In 2007 more than 1.7 million children had a parent in prison or jail."

THE SENTENCING PROJECT

CHAPTER 5
In a Family Way

—m—

The word "family" had many definitions for the women of Block 12, and none of them matched my middle-class, 1950s social model of having a mother, father, and children living together under one roof. For many of the inmates, family meant a mother and her children (not always of the same father) with a boyfriend or "ex" out there somewhere. It was also grandparents caring for grandchildren while mom was in her addiction or serving time. And, if a woman had not alienated everyone in her life, family meant weekly visits through closed-circuit television.

Sometimes a family consisted of a woman and her unborn baby until she gave birth in handcuffs and the child was taken away. This was the case with Angel who strolled into the barbershop one Wednesday evening without a nod or "hello." Eight other females followed her and waited while she chose where to sit. As soon as the guard slammed the metal door, the women squeezed into the green plastic chairs placed around the center table.

Angel picked up her chair and moved it to the corner of the crowded room, pushing it as far against the wall as she could. I was immediately intimidated by her size. She was much taller than the other women, broad in the shoulders, with a mop of curly red hair that stuck straight out from a center part and lacked the discipline of a brush. Her face was plain, almost masculine, with an angular jaw and straight thin lips that parted slightly to reveal missing front teeth. She had dark brown eyes, so large and beautiful they gave her pale face a startled look.

Once seated, Angel faced the door, tipped her chair slightly so it rested on its back legs against the concrete block and turned her head just enough to watch me.

I placed a stack of bright-colored composition notebooks on the table, along with pencils, index cards, and colored pencils. The women sat with their hands in their laps.

"Help yourselves," I said.

"Can we keep these?" Carla asked.

"Absolutely!"

They grabbed for the pile, trying to be polite. Each one chose a journal and pencils, then started to trade, like children passing out lunch-box snacks to get a better treat.

"I like blue. Can I have blue?"

"Here, I'd rather have stripes."

Maria made sure there were enough to go around. Samie asked Angel what color book she would like. She shrugged and didn't answer. Samie handed her an orange notebook and a pencil. Angel placed the items on her lap and faced the door again.

"My name is Linda," I said picking up the index cards and passing them around. "I'd like each of you to introduce yourself and make a name card. Fold the card in half so it stands up in front of you. It will help us get to know each other."

Marie wrote her name on a card and held it up for everyone to see. "I'm Marie. I've been coming to the writing class for about a month. It's fun."

Carla decorated her card with a pink flower and green squiggly lines around her name. She smiled at me and placed it in front of her. "I'm Carla."

Samie giggled, "Hey! Why didn't I think of that?" She flattened out her card and dug into the box of colored pencils.

"Me, I'm Latonya. I been here before…got myself picked up when my boyfriend an' I had a fight…he threw me out the car door right on the street and the cops, they stopped me for no reason…said I was in violation…I don't know why they got me instead of him…he's the one done somethin' wrong…I shoulda never got in the car with him. Thank you."

The remaining women introduced themselves, all except Angel. There was a pause as the group waited for her to speak.

"Angel," said a voice from the corner. She glared at me, put her unused index card on top of her notebook, then turned her face back to the door.

MEDITATION

"Welcome," I continued. "For those of you who are new, we spend ten minutes, at the beginning of each class in a relaxation exercise. You have the option to just observe or you may participate at any level you choose. There are no "musts" in this group."

I started the CD player. Strains of guitar music and tropical rainforest bird sounds filled the room. At my instruction, some of the women began to take deep breaths and closed their eyes. Doors slammed. Guards shouted in the hallway, and I read the meditation in a soft monotone voice.

"Breathe in deeply, filling your body with oxygen all the way to your fingers and toes, then slowly begin to exhale, letting it out..."

Like many first-time visitors, Angel kept her eyes wide open. Jean and I had no expectations. We understood that trust was a gift to be earned. Samie, Marie, and Cindy inhaled and exhaled deeply with the music while my voice droned on. Eventually, a few others allowed themselves to relax, but Angel's brown eyes glared at me from the corner while she rocked back and forth tapping her chair against the wall.

Scared rabbit eyes, I thought.

The meditation continued, and ten minutes later, when the exercise was complete, most of the group members were noticeably rested.

Maria opened her eyes first. "I've been doing this when I go to bed. It helps me sleep," she said.

Samie nodded. "It ain't easy to get to sleep here. Some people's up all night talking and carryin' on. I prays, and God helps me go to sleep. That's what I do. If you got the blessin' of the Lord, you can sleep good."

TEDDY BEARS AND SALTINES

"I had a baby shower yesterday," said Carmen smoothing the coarse fabric of her orange scrubs to show me her full-term belly. I hardly knew this pretty Hispanic girl who sat beside me. She appeared to be twenty-five years old.

"What?" I asked, turning to her and trying to hear above the other voices competing for my attention.

"They gave me a baby shower yesterday. The women."

"Tell me about it." I said. The others stopped talking.

"Oh, they drew pictures of teddy bears and things and gave me saltine crackers and some other stuff from the canteen. It was so nice. And they cut out pictures from magazines—things they would buy for the baby, if they could. Strollers and stuff."

"Yeah," Chrisy giggled. "We told her all the gifts was waiting on eBay for her to click on when she got out."

Angel watched as the other women laughed at the joke.

"No matter how hard you try," Marie said pursing her lips to look serious, "You can't get that stuff from the canteen."

"Are you getting pre-natal care?" I asked

"Oh, yes," said Carmen. It took a month for them to take me to the doctor, but I had an appointment. I had my last baby in jail, too. I have five children waiting for me at home.

A SECRET

The following Sunday, I offered to help Chaplain Martha with morning services. A group of women were already standing together in the gym when we arrived. Angel hurried up to me towering over my five-foot frame and stepped into my space. I looked up at her and moved back sensing she could hold her own in a barroom fight. She came in closer and bent down so we were eye-to-eye.

"I have to talk to you next Wednesday night," she whispered. "I'm pregnant and I'm going to prison. You gotta help me find someone to adopt my baby."

Then she turned and walked away, as if our meeting was mere chance.

On Wednesday, Angel was first in line coming through the classroom door. She took a chair beside me while the other women found their seats.

"I can't make any phone calls from here," she whispered. "Could you contact some adoption agencies and tell them what I want? I'll need their addresses, some envelopes, and paper to write to them."

I hesitated and did a mental review of my jail orientation. "Inmates *use* people," the officer had cautioned us. "They'll ask you for favors. Don't get involved in their personal lives!"

Sometimes I just couldn't help myself. Social workers have this gene that makes them want to fix people. It's written on our DNA. I weighed the options: cave in and help Angel, or follow the rules and tell her "no."

My common sense was on vacation that day. "I'll see what I can do," I said.

The following week, I made a few phone calls and consulted with my peers. We came up with a list of adoption agencies, addresses, and contacts. It was everything Angel asked for, everything she needed. I typed up the information and put it in an envelope. She had a right to her privacy.

Wednesday evening came, and I waited eagerly for class to begin. The women entered single file and chose seats around the table. Angel strolled in last and stood behind an empty chair at the opposite end of the room. When everyone else was seated she made an announcement.

"My sister and brother-in-law are going to adopt my baby!"

—〰—

"Women tend to commit less violent offenses, and are more known for committing what are commonly referred to as female offenses: prostitution, embezzlement, forgery, and counterfeiting."[6]

INSTITUTE FOR PUBLIC SAFETY AND JUSTICE FACT SHEET, 2001

CHAPTER 6
Our Girls

—⚇—

E very week there were new faces. The women went home or moved on to prisons and halfway houses, leaving space for the next batch of inmates to occupy their still-warm beds. Always there was change, but the block provided us with a constant supply of group members recruited by word of mouth and the promise of a free pencil and notebook.

On Wednesday nights we formed a family of sorts. Jean and I were the "moms" of Block 12 and privately referred to the inmates as "our girls." Regular group members hurried to sit next to us when they entered the room.

"Excuse me, that's my chair," was a common phrase at the beginning of class, but there were no arguments among the women over who got the preferred seats. Each understood her place in the social structure of the block, and those decisions were made long before they entered the classroom.

Women with longer sentences, who had earned the right to remain in Block 12 because of good behavior, often assumed leadership roles in the group. They were generally more mature than the average twenty-something inmate and a few had the advantage of being spiritually grounded. These leaders were a large part of the success of our group because they encouraged newcomers to attend and helped keep younger, more impulsive inmates in check.

MISS CARRIE

One of my personal favorites was a woman named Carrie. She was older than the others, possibly in her mid-fifties. She had the strong, calming presence of a loving mother and the women called her "Miss Carrie."

I first noticed Carrie's leadership role when other group members deferred to her choice of seats in the room. Over time, she moved to a place beside me. If it happened to be occupied when she entered the room, that person would simply get up and move to another chair at the table. The women respected her, and if one of them was the least bit noisy or disruptive, Miss Carrie would simply look at the offender until the behavior stopped.

Carrie's reputation also extended to her expertise in cooking. One Wednesday night following Easter, the women shared their gratitude for the ministry gift bags.

"Thank ya'll for the candy and hard-boiled eggs," said Angeline. "I was so happy to get a pink egg. You even put Easter grass in the bags. It works just like dental floss.

"Yeah, and Miss Carrie made deviled eggs," said Tamika.

"She makes really good deviled eggs," Karen added.

"Do you work in the kitchen?" I asked naively.

"Not...exactly," Carrie said, a smirk briefly crossing her lips. "We saved our mayonnaise and mustard packets."

A GIFT OF LOVE

I wanted to share my birthday with the women and e-mailed the captain to ask if I could bring a treat for the occasion. She called me the next day.

"Sharing your birthday would be a breach of the rules," she scolded. "Do you remember the discussion about proper boundaries when you went to your jail orientation?"

I apologized for the violation, embarrassed that I had to be reprimanded.

Miss Carrie planned a surprise birthday celebration for me anyway. She made a card that everyone signed, then led the group in singing "Happy Birthday." They threw handfuls of confetti into the air that had been secretly torn from colored magazine pages and concealed in the pockets of their scrubs. When the party was over, Miss Carrie picked up every scrap of paper in the room.

"Happy birthday," she whispered, pulling pieces from my hair.

"Thank you," I said, giving her a hug.

When I got home that evening, I discovered a single piece of hard candy in my jacket pocket. For eighteen months, Carrie was a mom to all of us, and when she left for prison, we all grieved the loss.

CODES OF CONDUCT

The women of Block 12 had their own rules, separate from those imposed by the jail. These rules passed from one inmate to another, nothing written down or even discussed, but understood and practiced by everyone, including Jean and me.

We used first names only, something like a twelve-step meeting in which anonymity is the goal, except no one required me to stand up and say, "Hi, I'm Linda and I'm a chocoholic."

So, when a woman asked, "Did you read about my case in the paper?" I could honestly say, "No" because I didn't know her last name. And if her face appeared on the front page, I didn't see it. My information came from radio and TV. Crimes committed by the women of Block 12 rarely made it to CNN.

It was important for the women to know how Jean and I felt about them. The question concerning an individual's notoriety was a test. Did we come to sit in judgment of her crimes? Would we turn away in disgust? So, each time I said, "No," I preserved the dignity of the inmate who asked the question. And each time there was an unmistakable look of relief that at least one person in the world didn't know how bad she really was.

Confidentiality was strictly observed. One evening, as Jean was passing out the nametags, Amanda said, "Kaitlin's not coming tonight."

"How come?" Jean asked.

"She's in Block 3 now."

"Oh. What happened?" Jean asked.

"She did something," Amanda replied without further explanation.

We simply did not ask questions about an individual's behavior or criminal history, and if one of the women chose to reveal something about her past, no one probed or encouraged her to say more.

I found this rule particularly difficult because it seriously interfered with my life as a practicing busybody, a sin I had struggled with as far back as I could remember. Keeping my mouth zipped had never been one of my personal strengths. In fact, I struggled with wanting to know everything about everyone else and then sharing it with the rest of the world. And each time it got me in trouble, I begged God to change me. He was doing just that. Women whose sins I perceived to be greater than my own were instructing me in the art of confidentiality.

Fourteen women living in a single room made it possible for an inmate to know everything about another individual, including the size of her underwear. Casual conversations overheard before and after the group implied a substantial network of shared information, but what went on inside the block stayed in the block. The women did not disclose what they knew about each other in front of Jean and me.

The inmates defended their right to attend groups as fiercely as they protected their privacy, and that meant strict obedience to the rules of the jail. Though I overheard comments from jail staff about the difficulty of working with female inmates and their unruly behavior in the block, this was not the case in our classroom. The women were polite and respectful, aware, of course, that microphones were tuned in to our conversations. They refrained from using profanity in our presence, and if a word just happened to "slip out," someone would gently reprimand the offender with, "We can't say that in here."

CONFLICT

One evening, two inmates entered the room and sat on opposite sides of the table.

"You been talkin' 'bout me," Mary said, pointing her finger at Sabrina.

Sabrina sat back in her chair with her arms folded across her chest and said nothing. The other women watched.

"I'm gonna git you for this. You ain't nothin' but trash!" Mary continued, her voice getting louder.

I was about to intervene when Sabrina looked at me. "Please call an officer," she said.

One of the women jumped up and pressed the call-button.

"Can I help you?"

Several inmates answered at once. "We need an officer in here."

Seconds later, two uniformed men unlocked the door. Mary shut her mouth.

"She's arguing with me," Sabrina explained to the officers.

"We'll need both of you to step out."

As the two were led away, Jo Ellen told us that both inmates would be punished for their participation. "That's the way it is," she said. "They've been fightin' all day."

I waited for someone to continue, hoping my curiosity would be satisfied with further tidbits of information.

The women pressed their lips together in silence. There was no gossip, no explanation, and no further discussion of the incident.

—m—

Discipline was rarely a problem. Even though most inmates were twenty-something, street smart, and immature, they adjusted quickly to our routine. Ninety minutes of prayer time, writing exercises, discussion, and group singing left little time for goofing off.

One young woman just couldn't help herself. Kara talked out of turn and giggled at inappropriate times. If we sang songs, she would raise her voice and sing off-key. Gentle reminders made no impression on her. I put up with her behavior for several weeks, thinking peer pressure would eventually settle her down. But it soon became apparent the other inmates didn't know what to do with her either.

Then, one night, when Kara was being particularly obnoxious, I decided to try a different approach. I took a deep breath and called on my stern mommy voice.

"If we continue to have interruptions," I said, "the class will end."

Kara kept talking to the person next to her as if she hadn't heard a thing. The other women waited to see what would happen. Jean and I packed up and called the guard to dismiss us.

The following Wednesday, Kara entered the room first and sat across from me. "Hey, ma'am," she said, slapping her hand on the table to get my attention, "I'm gonna be good."

---

*"In New York, a 1999 study of female inmates at Bedford Hills
Correctional Facility found that over 80% of women prisoners had a
childhood history of physical and sexual abuse, and more than 90% had
experienced physical violence or sexual assault during their lifetime."*[7]

INTERNATIONAL JOURNAL OF LAW AND PSYCHIATRY

CHAPTER 7

The Clothesline Project

—⚬—

A winter storm forced us to miss class for the first time. There was no direct way to tell the women, so I did the logical thing and called the jail to let them know about the cancellation.

"Central." It was a male officer who answered.

"This is Linda from the St. Vincent de Paul ministry."

"Who?"

"The jail ministry. I have a women's group tonight in Block 12. I need to cancel because of the weather."

"What's that again?" he asked, raising his voice.

"The women's group. Creative writing. Block 12. Could you let them know I won't be there?"

"Yeah, sure, I'll tell 'em," he said.

The line was dead before I could thank him.

Ministry groups were not a priority for the jail staff, but rather a disruption in the order of their day. On more than one occasion, Jean and I had to wait a half-hour or more to enter or leave the barbershop. Sometimes an officer would apologize and explained that organizations such as ours required extra personnel to make sure we were escorted safely through the building. Then they had to transport prisoners to and from meeting rooms and search them for contraband afterwards. All of these factors put a strain on our relationship with the staff.

A GUEST SPEAKER

I wasn't convinced the women would get my message, so I wrote letters to two inmates who had given me their last names: Carrie, the current group mentor, and Angel who now sat next to me at every opportunity. I explained the reason for our absence the night of the storm and reminded them we were scheduled to have a guest speaker the following week. I hoped they would help me out by encouraging the others to come.

Our speaker, Lori, was a counselor from the Women's Center, a local shelter. I'd met her earlier that year at a conference where the organization displayed its "Clothesline Project," a traveling exhibit of t-shirts designed by survivors of domestic violence.

The exhibit filled an entire room at the conference. Yards of clothesline were stretched between poles and arranged in neat rows reminiscent of a time when women hung their wash out to dry. Hundreds of colorful shirts dangled from clothespins, shirts painted with poems, word pictures, and simple phrases. As I walked along the rows, I read their stories, stories of nameless victims who had secrets to tell, and I wondered about the women who had enough courage to air their dirty laundry in public.

I wanted to share the "Clothesline Project" with the inmates. Up to that point, the women of Block 12 had not openly discussed their lives in relation to abuse, but I knew the statistics, and I suspected they applied to our group as well. Would they allow a stranger to speak to them about this subject or would they just stay away?

The following Wednesday, I met Lori in the jail lobby.

"I've never been to a jail before," she said quietly. "I'm a bit nervous."

I understood her fears and tried to reassure her. "The women in this group are non-violent offenders. They earn the right to attend based on their good behavior. I've never had any concerns about safety. The women love this group and don't want to lose the privilege of coming. Besides, officers are always watching us."

We checked in and were escorted to the barbershop. Lori and I took seats at opposite ends of the table. I wondered if Carrie and Angel had received my letters. Would our absence the week before affect attendance? Would the women stay away because of the sensitive nature of the subject?

A few minutes later, we heard voices, and through the window I saw a crowd of women coming down the narrow hallway. Carrie and Angel led the way with broad smiles and a "thumbs-up" gesture as they entered the room.

"Did they tell you I cancelled because of the weather last week?" I asked.

"Naw, but we figured it out," Carrrie said. "And we got your letters. Thanks for letting us know."

The group piled in and found seats around the table. We were short one chair, so Tami knocked on the window and asked the guard to bring us an extra. I waited for a moment of quiet to introduce our guest, but everyone was talking at once. Pictures were pulled out of notebooks and shirt pockets.

"Linda, here's one of Evan's latest pictures," said Angel handing me a snapshot of the new baby. "I brought these for you. My sister takes lots of them so I can see him grow."

"Here's my little girls," Felicia said, passing a wrinkled photo to the woman next to her. That's their Christmas picture from last year. They're bigger now, but I haven't seen them in four months. My mom won't bring them here." The pictures passed from hand to hand around the room. I reminded myself to pray for motherless children.

Tami was still waiting by the door. Another guard passed by.

"Knock on the window. She's real nice," said Carla.

Tami knocked again and within minutes the chair arrived.

T-SHIRTS

"Our guest speaker tonight is Lori." I said, when everyone was settled. "She is a domestic-violence counselor at the Women's Center."

"Thank you for inviting me to your group," Lori said, her voice barely above a whisper. "Does everyone here know about the Women's Center?" A few of the women nodded.

Lori passed out brochures. "We are a shelter for women and children who are victims of domestic violence. We offer counseling, childcare, assistance with finding a job, and we have an emergency number you can call twenty-four-hours a day if you need protection from an abusive relationship."

She opened a tote bag and carefully removed a stack of folded shirts. "This evening, I want to share something called our "Clothesline Project. These t-shirts were designed by victims and survivors of domestic violence. Normally, we display these shirts on a clothesline for viewing by the public, but because of limited space I brought a shirt for each of you to hold and look at. As you are passing the shirts around the table, please take one and place it in your lap while I read what the colors signify."

The women passed the shirts in silence.

"White is for a victim who has been murdered as a result of sexual or domestic violence." Lori read quietly.

"Red, pink, or orange, signifies a survivor of rape or sexual assault."

"Yellow or beige is a survivor or witness of domestic violence."

"Blue or green is someone who is a victim of incest or child sexual abuse."

"Purple or lavender represents a person attacked because they were thought to be gay or lesbian."

"Black or gray is a survivor of teen-dating violence."

"Now," Lori continued, "I want each of you to look at your shirt without saying anything. When you are ready, if you feel like sharing your shirt with the rest of the group, you may do so. You don't have to participate, if you don't want to."

Lori asked me to hold up my shirt and read the poem. It was a dark blue shirt denoting a survivor of incest or child sexual assault. The artist had decorated it with large spirals of glitter paint in vibrant hues of blue, green, and gold with blue, green, and red lettering.

I read, "This is for the children who cry themselves to sleep..."

The poem went on to talk about children who were afraid of Mommy and Daddy and afraid of their own homes.

CONFESSIONS

There was a moment of silence. Angel looked at me. "When I was twelve, my mother knocked my front teeth out," she said.

"I'm sorry that happened to you." Lori said softly. "Thank you for sharing with us."

Alyssa held up a yellow shirt representing domestic violence. Then she turned to me. "I used to lock my brother in the closet and take the beating myself so he wouldn't get hurt."

"You're very brave," I said.

"Thank you for sharing," Lori repeated.

Tamika held up a white shirt that showed one stick figure choking another. She looked around the room without saying a word, then folded the
shirt and placed it on the table in front of her.

Joanne's shirt had a tombstone with the name Jane Doe. "I was one
of the lucky ones," she said. "We didn't have any abuse in our family. I just
messed myself up on drugs."

Carmella's blue shirt had a woman's eyes with tears painted below them.
"I was sexually abused as a child," she said, turning away from Lori and
searching my face for approval. "My mother was an alcoholic, and she
couldn't take care of us, I know that. So, she sent us to live with our grandparents, knowing that our grandpa had molested my aunts and uncles. When
it happened to us, I told my grandma. She's hated me ever since."

"Thank you for sharing with us," Lori said softly.

Several women began to cry. Angel reached for tissues and began passing them to the others.

"My mom didn't protect me from my father and brothers," Julie said. "She
always said, 'Let 'em do whatever they want to you. They pay the bills.'"

"Everyone I have ever dated beat the crap out of me." It was Nancy who
spoke up. "What's wrong with me that I pick these violent and abusive men?"

"It isn't you, and it's nothing you have done," Lori answered. "All the
studies that have ever been done on victims of domestic violence have shown
only one common denominator: you are all women. There is no other factor.
Please remember, abuse is not about you—it's about *them*."

The stories and questions continued. As each woman spoke, she looked
at me as if to ask permission to tell her shameful secrets.

Samantha got up from the table and moved to the corner. She crouched
down and locked her arms around her knees in a fetal position. I went to sit
beside her on the floor.

"My momma had boyfriends," she whispered laying her head on my lap.
"And she let them have their way with me from the time I was six months old."
Her body began to tremble, and she let out a mournful cry. "I was a *baby*, for
God's sake!"

All I knew how to do was hold her. There were no words to ease her pain.

When Lori and I walked out of the jail into the cold winter night, she was shivering and visibly shaken. "There's so much pain in that little room," she said. "It's almost unbearable."

"You're right," I nodded. "So much pain and so much courage."

—ɱ—

"Religion defines evil and gives people the moral strength to resist."[8]

PHILIP YANCEY

CHAPTER 8
Faith Behind Bars

—⚏—

*P*rayer was never one of my strengths (maybe it's a Lutheran thing), but I've always admired a woman who could stand in front of a group with just the right-sounding words rolling off her tongue as if she got up that morning and God handed her a new psalm.

Not me. My prayers sounded more like begging with an occasional "thank you" thrown in to make sure I could return later with more requests. I rarely prayed out loud and never in front of others...until I met the women of Block 12.

They prayed about *everything*...

"God let there be peace in the block."

"Protect my family while I am away."

"I'm afraid I will die in prison."

"Lord, let the judge see that I'm serious about changing."

"Help my mother to forgive me."

"Jesus, take away my desire to use drugs and alcohol."

"Father God, care for all inmates, everywhere."

"Bless the guards and give them kind hearts."

"Thank you for sending Jean and Linda."

I, on the other hand, relied heavily on the Lord's Prayer, confident in my ability to say it out loud and with a group. So, at the end of each class, we joined hands and prayed.

"Our Father, who art in heaven…"

It sounded so "religious" when spoken in unison. It covered all the bases—praise, requests, thanksgiving, forgiveness. Jesus hadn't left anything out, and there was no need for me to come up with original material. I figured the praying part of class was covered. Then I discovered a person could get lost in a crowd of voices by mumbling to fit in.

I first noticed this one evening when we finished praying. Lana whispered to the woman next to her, "Don't worry, I'll teach you the words this week."

I went home that night, grieved by my lack of sensitivity. *Lord, what kind of Christian thinks everyone knows about Jesus and his famous prayer?* I typed up cards with words to the Lord's Prayer and added the Twenty-Third Psalm for good measure. It was a start, but it wasn't enough. I knew the women needed more than memorized words at the end of the group. The truth was they needed more than I could teach them.

SHARING THE GOSPEL

A lifetime of Sunday services did not prepare me for ministry at the jail. I was a Christian who thought going to church and doing a few good works was the equivalent of sharing the Gospel. The other stuff—leading Bible studies, asking people if they were saved, or praying out loud with someone—was the job of pastors and missionaries. I was simply not ready. But God knew that when he called me, and he made sure I got on-the-job training.

It didn't matter if the class was large or small or if the population of the block had turned over and every face was new. There were always one or two inmates who could quote scripture and were eager to share what they knew about the Bible.

One woman put it simply, "Doing time gives us time—to think and to pray. What else do we have to do in here?"

Because the women taught each other, there was a large network of believers that extended beyond the block to prisons and jails across the country. Some of the inmates had been incarcerated in several states. One of these was Veronica. I asked her about her prayer life and her ministry to others.

"As a kid, you don't know what the dynamics of prayer can do for you." Veronica said. "Your parents tell you to pray this way or that way and you do it. As I got older, I understood prayer better, and I used prayer for many aspects of my life. I'm always discussing something with God. A lot of times, I don't feel like praying because I don't think I'm getting anywhere. I'm impatient and not always consistent, but I do know God answers me. He knows us better than anyone else. He knows what our needs are. Without prayer, I don't know what I would do. You have to have something to believe in.

"You have to have your own daily conversation with him, and you need to be alone so you can pray in depth. God tells us to pray in secret, not publicly like the hypocrites. And he doesn't want us to pray selfish prayers. It's not all about us.

"When you pray, you should always go into a closet, or bathroom, or someplace private and close the door. When you pray to God in secret, he rewards you openly. If you really want to learn how to pray, go to the back of the Bible and look up the word 'prayer.' There are plenty of passages in scripture that teach us how and when to pray.

"We get so caught up in our addictions and the other things in life," she continued. "How we impact others is really important. If I can do something to help another person know Jesus, I will. I tell them, 'This is not me talking, but God. Go to the scripture and see for yourself.' God wants us to share His Word."

Another self-appointed mentor had been in and out of the system for more than twenty years when I met her. Lynn's personal relationship with God started in prison.

"When you're alone in your cell for twenty-three hours a day, you have this natural desire to communicate with your creator," she explained. "He makes himself so available to us, but sometimes he just has to get us alone where we can be quiet and listen to him. I start my day with prayer before I even get out of bed. Otherwise, it doesn't go well."

While incarcerated, Lynn turned her childhood suffering and addictions into hope for other women, using every opportunity to help others come to Christ. In one minimum-security prison, she taught an arts and crafts class so she could share the Gospel with women who didn't attend church services or Bible studies.

"When I came to the jail," one inmate told me, "Lynn taught me how to read. Now I can read and understand my Bible."

Each mentor found a way to help others. Didi, a baby-faced woman in her mid-thirties who made no effort to hide the fact that she sucked her thumb, spoke boldly of her own prayer life. "I organize the women to pray every night before bedtime," she said. "That way, no one is afraid to go to sleep."

For every inmate willing and able to teach others about God, there were five more who had no idea who he was. Jean and I discovered a woman's initial exposure to the belief in a power greater than herself often coincided with her first incarceration. Bible studies, twelve-step programs, and church services, combined with the efforts of inmate mentors, offered more opportunities to hear the Gospel behind bars than on the street.

Very few women mentioned previous church attendance or religious education.

"I was invited to church once," a middle-aged woman confessed to us. "It was at the First Assembly of God. They were offering free cappuccino, and being of the criminal mind, I accepted."

Once institutionalized, the inmates were a captive audience for ministry groups because they craved the attention of anyone who would listen to them. The loneliness and confinement of a jail cell was ideal soil for planting God's word, and it might also be the only time an inmate was sober and clear thinking enough to process what she heard. Holding on to that information and applying it to her daily life was more of a challenge.

UNCONDITIONAL LOVE

"It's easy to live for God on the inside when you don't have the influences of the world," Lynn said. "I've seen so many women who are hurting and lost. They try to fill a void with alcohol, drugs, men, cigarettes, gambling, or other women. But they are looking for something only God can provide. I tell them the Good News—God hasn't given up on them and he never will."

The message was simple but hard to sell. Many of the women were strangers to the concept of unconditional love because they had suffered so much.

"My father is an alcoholic," Beverly told us. "He used to have a terrible temper. I remember once, when I was about ten, he beat me for spilling a glass of milk. He beat me so bad I had to stay out of school for a month until the bruises healed. My uncle lived down the street from us, and when he saw me, he walked over to our house and threatened my dad. He said, 'If you ever lay a hand on that girl again, I'm gonna kill you!' My father doesn't drink anymore, and we are working on our relationship. I'm trying to forgive him, but I can't forget."

I wanted to fix the women and take away their pain. I wanted them to believe in God, but I lacked the skills to teach them how.

What is my role in this ministry, Lord? I asked.

Just tell them, I love them, he said.

So Jean and I told Bible stories. The women sat before us in silent wonder as if they had never heard them before. Even the birth of baby Jesus with the wise men, shepherds, and angel choir was news to some of them. We talked about God's love for sinners like King David and Moses in the hope they would understand the concept of forgiveness. And every time we told the inmates they were created in God's image and loved beyond their comprehension, they stared at us in disbelief.

"But we've done bad things," they would say.

"We've all done bad things," I answered. "There is something broken in each of us, and God loves us even when we can't love ourselves."

PRAYER AND FASTING

The group was always hungry for more information. They loved to read out loud and discuss books by authors like Joyce Meyer. One night, I asked the women what they would like to study next. Amanda suggested we find a book on prayer. The vote was unanimous.

I chose *The Power of a Praying Woman* by Stormie Omartian. The ministry bought ten copies, and the captain gave the women permission to take them back to the block for reading. Their favorite chapter dealt with ways to defeat the enemy. Prayer and fasting became a hot topic in Block 12.

"When I was about twelve," Francine said, " I remember fasting. It was something we had to do. My mother was very religious. I just remember being hungry and wanting food."

"I tried fasting once," Octavia said proudly. "The last time I was in here, Veronica got me to do it. She was always ministering to us and praying with us. One day, she suggested that we fast and pray together about some of the issues I had going on at the time. We did it. Every time the others were eating,

Veronica and I went into the bathroom and prayed together. That took away the hunger and, oh, the power of that! I didn't realize it at the time it was going on, but that was very effective prayer."

I thought about what the women were saying. "Okay," I said. "I could use effective prayer *and* a few less calories. I'll take the challenge and fast one day this weekend, and I'm going to journal through it. If any of the rest of you decide to join me, please don't go back to the block and say, 'Linda said we have to fast!'"

The women laughed. "Don't worry," Ruth said, "We can keep a secret."

I lasted twenty-three hours, the longest I'd ever been without food. The day went pretty much as Octavia had predicted. I drank water. When I was hungry, I prayed and immediately the hunger was gone. I prayed for the women and found I was able to actually listen and be silent before God—a challenge under normal circumstances.

The following Wednesday, I announced my success. "Twenty-three hours!" It seems I'd forgotten Veronica's admonition to "pray in secret."

Octavia, Karen, and Ruth grinned at me. "Forty-eight," Ruth said quietly. "I spent all my waking hours in the Word," Octavia said. "It was powerful."

"Did anyone have trouble with the guards?" I asked.

"No, we didn't," said Ruth.

"The first day at breakfast," Julie reported, "one of the CO's told me to go in the bathroom and tell those three women, 'Its time to eat.' Then he asked, 'What are they doing in there anyway?' I told him, 'They're having a religious experience!'"

—w—

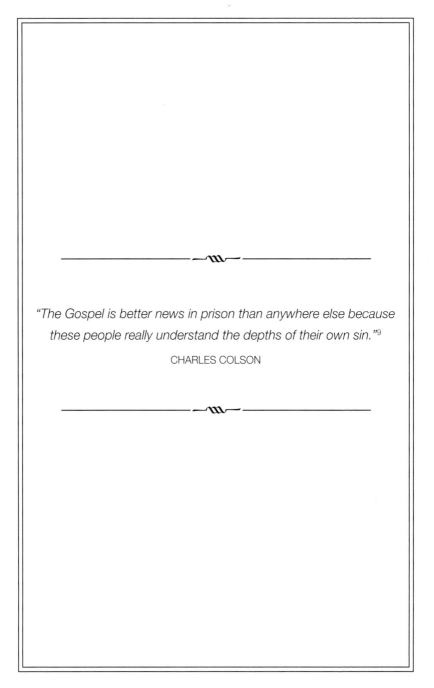

"The Gospel is better news in prison than anywhere else because these people really understand the depths of their own sin."[9]

CHARLES COLSON

CHAPTER 9
Let's Shout to the Lord

—⁓—

Thirty years ago, I met a woman whose ministry now flows through me and blesses people she will never meet. Her name was Char and she led a women's group at the church I was attending. There were ten of us, young moms struggling with the issues of raising families, and we gathered on Thursday evenings to pray and sing. Char was our prayer mentor, and she taught us how to praise God with words and music.

Char had a beautiful voice. She would say a prayer and then teach us a song while she strummed the chords on her autoharp—prayer, song, prayer, song—until the petitions of everyone in the room were brought before the Lord.

Char made sure we had copies of her music. I stored mine in the bottom of the piano bench, occasionally digging them out to console a fretful child or sing myself through a hard day. Sometimes, those songs brought comfort when nothing else could.

I thought the women of Block 12 might like to hear Char's music, so I bought myself an easier, electronic version of the autoharp (a Q-Chord), practiced for a few months, and took it to the Wednesday night group.

"Would you like to sing?" I asked.

"Yeah, I love to sing. What kind of songs you got?"

"Naw, I can't sing! You sing for us."

"Hey, what's that thing called? How do you play it? "

"How much did it cost?"

When all of their questions were answered, Jean passed out copies of the lyrics. From that day forward, we ended the class with songs of praise, and the women often told us it was the best part of our time together.

I LOVE TO TELL THE STORY

Over the years, I added to Char's list until we had a large collection of contemporary and traditional hymns, as well as songs from youth ministries. I wondered if Sunday school and Bible camp songs were appropriate for women who ranged in age from eighteen to sixty, but it wasn't long before we discovered most of them loved to hear a Bible story, set to music, even the street-smart little girls with bad attitudes.

The strict enforcement of drug laws brought us young women, teens and twenty-year olds whose lives were caught up in the world of gangs and pimps. I could spot them when they walked in the door and refused to look at me, their faces frozen into a continuous scowl. They showed up for the free stuff, a pencil and pad of paper handed out at the beginning of class, then sat with arms crossed and heads down waiting for the group to end.

Occasionally, one was brave enough to say, "I don't believe in God."

"It's okay," I would tell her. "We're just glad you're here."

If the girl came back, I knew she was just a little bit curious and maybe there was something in our lesson for the day or in the music that interested her.

Songs like *El Shaddai* gave Jean and me the opportunity to pause and share a Bible lesson. We talked about the many names of God and his everlasting love for his people. Even those inmates who claimed to be atheists lifted their heads to listen to the story of Abraham and Isaac and how Abraham had such faith he was willing to sacrifice his only son.

"God provided a wild ram in Isaac's place," we explained to the women. "And he has provided Jesus to take your place."

Some songs gave the women an opportunity to exercise their leadership qualities. Such was the case with Heather, a young lady who lived at the jail for almost two years. She was a leader, all right, but not in the positive sense—until she discovered the song "Dem Bones."

Heather loved to read out loud and enjoyed this humorous version of the creation story. She was a master at acting out the parts of God, Adam, Eve, and the Devil. The women always asked to sing "Dem Bones" first and would beg Heather to lead the song while they joined in with "Dem bones gonna rise again."

I'd like to think our music and praise sessions had something to do with Heather's transformation, but we can't take all the credit. There was work going on behind the scenes. Inmate mentors and jail ministry people prayed with and for Heather and the change, when it finally occurred, was nothing short of a miracle. This angry young woman who had spent her teen years running with the wrong people turned her life over to Jesus and began to lead others to faith.

DRUMMING

Like Char's music so many years ago, the praise and worship part of Wednesday night group became a time of joy and healing for all of us. With the help of a music therapist and the permission of the captain, we added drumming to our program. A larger room was also provided for our use. The ministry purchased a variety of drums and percussion instruments, and we started a monthly circle led by several women from the community. At first, the inmates were reluctant to join in, but when they discovered it was a no-talent-necessary program, the enthusiasm grew. We were very loud! The officers and the male inmates sometimes complained, but we had a lot of fun. The young volunteers brought life and enthusiasm to the group, adding dances, songs and new opportunities for prayer.

GIVE HIM EVERYTHING

One particular song became an all-time favorite of the women. *Give Him Everything*, by Beki Hemmingway Kerkman,[10] was originally recorded for children. We sang the song in a call and response format with the group divided in two parts.

Group A would sing the first part and Group B would echo.

(chorus)
Give him everything. Give him everything.
Give him everything. Give him everything.

Then everyone sang:
Jesus loves the gifts we bring, so let's give him everything.

Widow in the church. Widow in the church
Gave her two cents worth. Gave her two cents worth.
It was all she had on earth, so she gave her everything.

Boy with fish and bread. Boy with fish and bread
Did what Jesus said. Did what Jesus said.
With his lunch five thousand were fed, and he gave his everything.

Now, all of us have talents. All of us have talents.
And treasures we can share. And treasures we can share.
God can use us anywhere if we give him everything.

One Wednesday evening, the women hurried into the classroom, giggling and excited. Several were carrying sheets of paper.

"We have a surprise for you!" one of the women shouted. "Tonight, when we sing *Give Him Everything*, don't stop playing. We're gonna sing some extra verses!"

"Can we do it right now?" another asked.

I pulled out the Q-chord, and the whole class started to sing.

"Give him everything . . ."

When the song came to the end, I continued to play. Three women stood up to perform.

Inmate in the jail. Inmate in the jail
Didn't make her bail. Didn't make her bail.
She went to creative writing, and she gave her everything.

She's stuck in Pod 3. She's stuck in Pod 3*
In her misery. In her misery.
Until she sang on Wednesday nights, now she gives her everything.

With her pencils and paper. With her pencils and paper
Correspondence will save her. Correspondence will save her.
Keeps in touch with family and friends as she gives her everything.

Reading in God's Book. Reading in God's book
Gives a good outlook. Gives a good outlook.
Keeps us focused on our lives as we give our everything.

*Author's note. The women were living in another cellblock at the time this song was written.

All of the women cheered and squealed with delight when the song ended. It was very difficult to play an autoharp and cry at the same time.

IN HIS HANDS

If you've never lost your freedom, it's hard to grasp the idea of constant surveillance. Everything we said, everything we did was a performance for the control room.

Ministry volunteers would often joke, "Don't ever scratch or do anything embarrassing. Someone is watching."

This was a good thing. It ensured our safety. And it gave us an opportunity to share the music with others. One night as we sang *Let There Be Peace On Earth* and I struggled to keep up with the difficult chord changes, a beautiful baritone voice joined in. Jean later told me a male officer was standing outside our room with his hands folded in front of him, singing along.

Of course, the inmates were always tuned in to the fact that they were being watched and sometimes, they wanted to have a little fun. They liked to make up verses to *He's Got the Whole World in His Hands*.

"He's got Block 12 in his hands."

"He's got the judge and the jury in his hands."

"He's got probation and parole in his hands."

"He's got all of our families in his hands."

One night, Heather whispered, "Officer Smith is having a bad day. He's been real crabby to us. We can't sing, can't laugh. How about we sing 'He's got Officer Smith in his hands?'"

The group took their voices up a notch, "He's got CO Smith in his hands. He's got CO Smith in his hands. He's got CO Smith in his hands. He's got the whole world in his hands."

Silence.

Heather was the first to speak. "We're really screwed."

"I think Officer Smith needs a hug," said Samantha laughing. "You handle it, Heather."

KUMBAYA

Most nights we sounded just awful, no reflection on my musical talents of course. I struggled with the chords, the women sang off-key, and we could get a bit loud and obnoxious. But then, other times, if you listened carefully, well...things happened and the whole mood would change...like the night we sang for Alethea.

It started out like any other Wednesday. Eight women filed into the barbershop. Among them was a young woman in her early twenties who had been with us for six months. Alethea was withdrawn and rarely contributed to class. Most nights she sat with her head down, just listening. Her neck and arms were covered in gang tattoos, a palette of swastikas, stars, names, and symbols I didn't recognize. More troubling were the dark brown scars that crisscrossed her arms disrupting the underlying designs. Like so many of the young inmates, Alethea was a cutter who mutilated her body to ease emotional pain.

When I handed her the class materials, Alethea used them to cover her face. I asked if she was tired.

"I have some problems I'm dealing with," she answered.

"Would you like to talk about them?"

She shook her head, "No, I'll start crying."

An hour later, I passed out song sheets. Alethea covered her face with the paper again and leaned toward me to speak privately.

"I'm going to court on the fifteenth," she whispered. "I'm looking at twenty years." Tears welled up in her eyes, and she looked away.

It was difficult to move on, but I knew she didn't want to be the center of attention. I nodded to Jean. She picked up a pack of tissues, took a seat beside Alethea, and wrapped her arms around her.

We began to sing. The women were subdued, calling out their favorite songs in hushed tones.

"Let's sing Amazing Grace."

"How about Jesus Loves Me?"

No one laughed at their mistakes or clapped when a song ended. That night the music was perfect, and their voices blended into a beautiful lullaby. And I thought about the angel choir that gathered in the skies over Bethlehem.

"Kumbaya, Lord (come by here)."

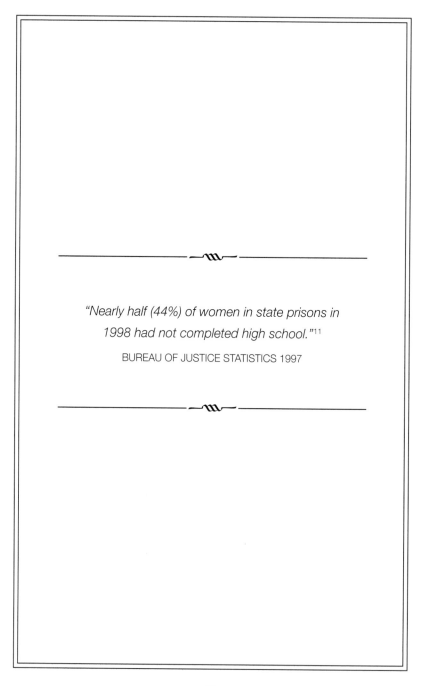

"Nearly half (44%) of women in state prisons in 1998 had not completed high school."[11]

BUREAU OF JUSTICE STATISTICS 1997

CHAPTER 10
Jailhouse Ingenuity

—◦◦◦—

"I have a favor to ask you," I said one evening at the beginning of class. The women stopped talking and listened.

"Over the past few years, I have been working on a book about my experiences in this group." I paused to study their faces wondering if they would reject me after this confession.

"I'm doing this because I want people to get to know you and understand why you are here. Our society puts men and women in jails and prisons, and then we forget about them. It's kind of an 'out of sight, out of mind' mentality.

"We don't really know who you are. We don't understand your needs, and we don't listen to what you have to say. As a matter of fact, most people aren't interested in what inmates have to say. We focus on our own opinions, what the neighbors think, and what the news media feeds us about crime and criminals.

"I'd like to change that. You all have voices that should be heard. Just like when you're drumming, I want to hear your voices. I want the reader to understand who you are, why you're here, and what we can do to help you."

"We're listening," said Jamie.

I wondered if the control room was listening, too. Would someone report I had over-stepped my professional boundaries again by giving out personal information such as the fact that I was a writer? Oh, well, with any luck, if I broke enough rules, I could probably get the material I needed first-hand.

"The section I'm working on now is about jailhouse ingenuity," I continued. "You're always telling me how you make do with what you have—for example, using toothpaste to keep braids from unraveling. I think this information would be both interesting and humorous for the reader, and I was hoping you'd help me write this chapter."

Everyone started to talk at once.

"Toothpaste can be used for a lot of things."

"What about plucking eyebrows?"

"Hey, Jan taught us how to make great burritos."

I put up my hand. "Hold on! I need a piece of paper and a pencil."

Two women shoved the necessary tools in my direction, and they all started talking again. This is what they had to say.

CANTEEN

Block 12 is a privilege block, which means the women are allowed to purchase items from the canteen. These include necessities such as Tylenol, Tums, shampoo, baby oil, toothpaste, deodorant, and other personal care products. The food items available include, but are not limited to, instant coffee, ramen noodles, beef sticks, flavored drink mixes, chips, and candy. Inmates must have money in an account to purchase these products. Family and friends can make deposits to supplement an account.

If an inmate is indigent, they are not able to get canteen items, but they are given two envelopes with stamps (weekly), deodorant, a comb, toothbrush and toothpaste, a pack of Tylenol, Tums, and a small bar of soap. All inmates receive two changes of underwear and scrubs per week, one blanket, a sheet, and a pillowcase.

The block also has an ice machine and microwave. The jail ministry provides coffee pots for hot water in each housing unit. With these luxuries, the women have created ways to "make do."

HAIR CARE

Hairspray: Dip a toothbrush in sugar water. Hold it several inches from your hair. Run your thumb over the bristles to create a spraying action.

Clear toothpaste will hold the ends of braided hair in place.

Curlers: Roll hair around tampons. Wrap the tampon string around to secure in place. Baby oil works as a setting lotion.

BEAUTY AND COSMETICS

Piercing: Teeth from combs are broken off and used to pierce eyebrows and ears. The comb is left in place as jewelry.

Mascara: Mix clear toothpaste, water, and colored pencil. Use a toothbrush to apply.

Salt and baby oil rubbed on the skin works as an ex-foliant.

Toothpaste applied to pimples reduces the redness.

Skin bronzer: Coffee and body lotion provide a tan.

Eye shadow and foundation: These products are made by crushing colored Tums, not the canteen brand but the good ones provided by the nurse. One inmate was known for her expertise in mixing Tums with lotion to produce various shades of make-up.

The inside of an orange peel rubbed over nails softens and conditions the cuticles.

Eyebrow grooming: Pull a thread from your sock. Tie the ends together to form a circle. Twist circle several times to form a figure eight. Hold one looped end in each hand. Pull the loops back and forth while holding over the area to be plucked. The twisting of the thread will catch on the hairs and pull them out.

PERSONAL HYGIENE

Earplugs: Save plastic wrap from sandwiches in bag lunches. Make two small balls from sanitary napkins. Wrap tightly in plastic wrap. Place in ears. Works better than store-bought.

Dental floss: Made from thread removed from clothing or sock.

Shower head: When shower spray is weak, hollow out an empty toothpaste tube. Cut off the top, leaving several inches of tube. Slip over showerhead to force water into a stronger stream.

Heating pad: Save empty plastic soda bottle and fill with hot water from coffee pot.

Laundry Soap: Save a plastic bag. Add a small bar of soap and hot water. Squish until soap is liquid. Use to wash out underwear.

Insoles: Remove paper strip from sanitary napkin pads. Place in shoes to make them softer and more comfortable. This also absorbs foot odor.

Tampons (not provided in some jails): Use sanitary napkins. Tear into strips. Twist and use as tampons.

ARTS & CRAFTS

Jailhouse scissors: Using a pencil, trace a design over and over on a piece of paper until the paper is worn thin, and you can pull it apart. You can make a stencil by this method.

Toothpaste works as a substitute for glue.

Tampon art: Tear off wads of cotton from a tampon. Dip in baby oil. Rub vigorously over a color on a magazine page. Dab on paper to create painted designs or stencils.

Erasers: Use the soles of tennis shoes to erase pencil marks.

RECIPES

Popsicles: Sprinkle Kool-aid over ice cubes.

Iced or hot tea can be flavored with Kool-aid.

Chili popcorn: Sprinkle seasoning packet from chili-flavored ramen noodles over popped popcorn.

Cappuccino: Break up butterscotch candy. Add a cup of hot water to dissolve. Add instant coffee, hot cocoa, and sugar. Add ice for cold drink.

Jailhouse burritos: Crush a bag of Doritos being careful not to break the bag. Open bag and add hot water, cheese, seasoning packet from chili-flavored ramen noodles, and pieces of spicy beef sticks. Fold top of bag over to close. Place under mattress for 10 minutes to cook. Serve with Doritos or Fritos.

Hooch: This is a very potent alcoholic beverage. The women assured me they had only heard about it, never made it or experienced its effects. We are giving only a partial recipe.

Hooch Recipe

Save a soda bottle. Fill with water.

Add:

    Flavored drink mix

    Sugar

    Crumbled slice of bread (for the yeast)

    Orange peel

Mix all ingredients together and hide for 1 month.

Two shots and you're good.

Serves a crowd.

"To imprison a woman is to remove her voice from the world, but many female inmates have been silenced by life long before the transport van carries them from the courthouse to the correctional facility." [12]

WALLY LAMB

CHAPTER 11

P.O. Box 666

—ɯ—

One Saturday morning, I walked into the post office in downtown Mukwonago, Wisconsin, eager to rent my very first P.O. box. Some of the women had asked if they could write to me when they went home or moved on to prison.

I paid the rental fee, and the clerk handed me a key.

"Your number is 666," he said.

I stared at him without blinking, my mouth open and poised to say something really intelligent like, "Excuse me, sir, could you choose another number? I really don't think the sign of the beast would work for a jail ministry."

But my assertive self wasn't up to it, so I grabbed the key and hurried away from the service counter, pretending it didn't matter. Box 666 was on the far wall of the post office about waist high. It looked exactly like the others. There were no flame marks around the edges, and the metal door was cool to the touch, so I put the key in the lock, opened it a crack, and peeked inside. There was a six-by-six inch view into the mailroom.

"Nothing unusual here," I said to the empty cubicle. Satisfied, I closed and locked the door.

"You aren't the superstitious type," I mumbled under my breath as I walked to the car. "It's just a number. 'Greater is he that is in you than he who lives in the world.'" (1 John 4:4).

And that's exactly what I tell the women when they look at the address on my business card and say, "Huh?"

I tell them, "God is in control!"

Since that day, P.O. Box 666 has brought me a world of blessings. Tucked in among stacks of post office junk mail, colorful grocery-store flyers, and coupons to steam clean three 9x12 carpets for only $99.99 are treasures in the form of cards and letters from women who have been in our group—and friends of theirs who have not.

I keep all of their letters and answer every one. Some of them continue their correspondence throughout the time of their incarceration and beyond. The collection now fills a large box. The letters serve to remind me how God takes our little gifts, the seeds that we plant in the name of ministry, and makes them grow into beautiful gardens of blessings. To preserve the privacy of these individuals, I have not included their real names or any other information that would reveal their identities.

Sometimes a letter comes from a woman who has not had a chance to say goodbye.

Dear Linda
I woke up at 5:15 am yesterday. I knew it was my day to leave for prison, even though no one had told me. The CO came in and said I had 15 minutes to pack. Carrie got up with me and said goodbye. I promise to write when I get settled. *Angel*

Inmate Communication Form
To: St. Vincent de Paul ladies
Subject: I just wanted to let you know I have been granted time served. I am probably home already. Thank you for all you do for us. God bless you. *Randi*

Linda & Jean,
It is so nice to be able to go outside and feel the fresh air. The building is set up on a hill. The grounds are peaceful and very green. It was an eye-opener for me. I thought, "The women live part of their lives here, or even a lifetime—working, going to school, and building some kind of foundation for themselves. They learn to endure, have strength and faith, all seemingly content on these college-campus-like grounds. The only thing deterring them from the outside world is the fence surrounding them. Freedom is so close, yet unattainable. *Skye*

I arrived at the prison two weeks ago. I still have not heard anything about how my children are doing. My mother did finally write me and said she was glad I was working on my problems instead of running. *Monica*

—⟋⟍—

Truthfully, I'm doing okay. Today is one week I've been here and I still haven't heard from my family. So, I'm feeling pretty lonely, somewhat forgotten about, and expendable. I'm having a little pity party, but I've been giving quite a bit of time each day to praying and reading my Bible. *Sam*

Thank you for your letters. I am okay here, but the days are long, and I really appreciate you writing to me. It seems your letters just come at the right time, when I need them most. I'll be here for a long time, and I would like to start a ministry. I want to help people the way St. Vincent de Paul has helped me. *Jodi*

Thank you for the beautiful poems. I have them taped to my cabinet, and I will keep them forever. My cellmate is a very nice woman who has had a terrible life. She is so depressed and feels that all is hopeless. I just repeat to her the things you taught us in class. You have no idea how far your work reaches to others. *Larissa*

Thank you for the card. I took the inspirational message you sent me and passed it on to another inmate in the AODA program. I wrote on the back for her to keep it as long as she needs to be "reminded," and then to pass it along to yet another person in need. Linda, your thoughtfulness is so greatly appreciated and valued. I am driven by you to spread the word and share what you give. *Shana*

I am touched and inspired by how well you remembered me and my individual circumstances. Your support and encouragement is unwavering and gives me great hope for my healing and the future. *Jessie*

I've been home for two months and am sharing an apartment with a friend. My most exciting news! I'm joining a group at church. It's a praise and singing group that goes to prisons. I can't wait. Thanks to you and Jean and God, I can connect my love for God to prisoners like myself. You two inspired me, and I thank you for that. *Jade*

You fill my life with joy and laughter. Smile, God loves you and so do I. *Mary*

I'd just like to say "Thank-U" for being there when I knew I didn't have a human in my life that cared about me because I have been locked up and I have no one but good, understanding Jesus, my children, and a friend like

91

you to write to every once in awhile. *Kim*

When I get out, do you think you could help me as far as work? I know you work at a nursing home, and I could work maybe food service or housekeeping. I would appreciate it. I know it's some ways away. But I know I might have a chance. I would maybe like to work with you at the jail. These things might not happen, but it's a goal. *Angie*

When I came to the jail, I saw no way out. I had been drinking almost daily for eighteen years and was a completely broken person. You came faithfully on Wednesday nights, no matter what, to spend time with us—the inmates. How I looked forward to seeing you and listening to you and singing the songs. It was as if you helped to nurture my broken soul. While I listened and saw the joy of the Lord within you, there was a healing taking place. I thank you for that hope and the desire you gave, the seed you planted with your caring and kindness. *Lana*

An acquaintance of mine, who served time in a Federal prison, taught me how to get the most mileage out of cards sent to inmates.

"A greeting card is like a gift," she said. "Prisoners don't often have access to them. Buy or make a card that fits a business-size envelope, then sign it in pencil. Unsigned cards are considered contraband by prison officials and will be rejected."

I soon learned the value of this practice when I received the following letter:

Thank you for writing to me and for the beautiful cards. I selfishly keep them for a while and then erase your name and use them over again. That's okay, isn't it? I hope you don't mind. How do you like this cute wrapping paper? I got it free from a company that sent me a calendar at Christmas time. I can use the back to write letters on. *Sylvia*

After Miss Carrie left Block 12 to go to prison, she wrote the following letters:

December 2005

Hi Linda & Jean,

Surprised? Yeah, me too! I thought I'd have a little more time with you. Anyway, I want to say "thank you" to both of you for being so kind to me. You and Jean have been, warm, kind, and most of all, non-judgmental. What you gave me helped more than you know. I am at the Federal Transfer Center on my way to Dublin, California. I will miss our weekly meetings and the songs you play. I will keep the two of you in my prayers! I miss you both already. It

92

is extremely overcrowded here, about 1400 women in a prison designed for 800. Jobs are limited and everyone starts out working in the kitchen for $5.25 per month for the first two months. It gradually goes up to about $25 a month depending on your job assignment—unless you work in the prison industry.

January 2006

The job I was going to tell you about is something new here at this facility. The institution has contracted with a private company to provide telephone operators to field 411 calls. The operation isn't off the ground yet but is supposed to be by the end of the month. To start, I will make $0.23 an hour. After about a month, providing I pass the probationary period, that will increase to $0.46 an hour. They have five pay levels all together, but it takes awhile to get beyond the $0.46. It's sad, but right now that is sounding pretty good. Everything at the commissary is high. The company representatives will be here next week to train us. That will last a week. Then we will get tested. After we pass the test, we become AGENTS. That's what they tell me anyway. I'll keep you posted.

February 2006

The job is coming along okay. I get up at 3 am, my escort arrives about 3:45 am, and I'm at my station ready to log on at 3:59:30. I try to be in bed by 8 pm but it doesn't always happen. So, I've been experimenting with afternoon naps. They seem to help. I call them power naps.

March 2006

Yes, I remember when we fasted. It was the first time I had ever done anything like that. And, since you reminded me of it, I think I'll do it again. I don't know if God did anything special for me that he doesn't already do, but as J. said, "It's a way of giving back." Or, more so for me, a way of saying "thank you" to Him. Now that I know it's okay to drink water, I may even shoot for a day-and-a-half!

March 2006

...I'm hanging in here. The days have picked up their pace and seem to be passing quickly. I work five days a week, 7.25 hours a day, and try to put in at least three or four hours on my off days. For the past month, my shift has been 4 am to 11:45 am. Once I get past the part of getting up, I'm okay. Of course, I'm working for slave wages but at least I can buy my necessities now, and it passes the time. The call center here is one of several that the company owns. We answer directory assistance calls, so although the work is not hard, it is sometimes stressful. You'd be surprised how many rude and ornery people there are in the world.

April 2006

Easter crept by virtually un-noticed here. They are a little backwards when it comes to programming. Example: there's a special program scheduled for Cinco de Mayo, but there was none for Easter. Go figure.

May 2006

I hope you had a good Mother's Day. Me? I'm okay. My day was decent. A few of the women and myself got together in honor of the day and shared some food. You'd be surprised what you can do with a microwave and the few staples that we have access to. There were potato roll-ups, macaroni & cheese, fried rice, nachos and cheese, tuna casserole. And then, there were the desserts! Cheesecakes, custard, chocolate pudding with strawberry and banana cut up in it, and fruit salad made with whipped cream. Not bad, huh?

July 2007

I had to share this with you. We had a concert today. Not only is the woman's name Linda, but she plays a harp. It's different than yours, the kind that stands on the floor, with strings. The first song she played was "El Shaddai." The second was "Do Lord." It felt like you were here with me.

March 2008

As for now, I'm working a lot of hours and trying to save as much money as I can. My Scrabble playing is down to about one day a week. Some days, when I come in, I only have enough time to shower before I go to bed. The down-side to this is I don't get to write as often as I'd like to. But there's one thing for certain and that is I keep you in my prayers daily. I pray while I'm in the shower.

June 2008

It's quite warm here, which personally I like, but I'm indoors most of the day so I don't get to enjoy it as much as I'd like. Right now, I go out about three times a week and walk the track. I only walk about a mile because of controlled movement. What is controlled movement? Well, someone came up with the bright idea that allows us to go and come from point A to point B in ten minutes—only on the half-hour, each hour. So when you go someplace, you have to stay there for at least an hour. Things have really changed here and not for the better.

January 2009

Things around here have become pretty solemn. We have a new warden who has no humanitarian streak. Just when you thought things couldn't get much worse, he showed us we were wrong. Last year (before him) we had a few choirs come in around Christmas time. This year, we had none. We used to decorate our doors, not this year. I am thankful this was my last Christmas here, but I can't help but feel for those who will have to remain.

August 2009 – released

I left Dublin at 8 am, Thursday, the 14th, and was scheduled to arrive in Jacksonville at the halfway house by 11:30 pm the same night. Scheduled, because it didn't happen. The whole trip turned out to be a test, and I am thankful to be able to say I passed it. The information that the institution gave me was sketchy at best. They really need to revise their procedures. Anyway, I took the BART (Bay Area Rapid Transit) to the airport. It's about an hour trip. Halfway there, I realized I didn't have a ticket. So I go to the ticket counter, tell the person I'm there to pick up my ticket that was purchased by the Bureau of Prisons. She asks for ID, and all I have is my prison inmate ID. I show her this and she says she can't take that, do I have a credit card. After getting a tight reign on my composure, I explain that I have just been released from Federal prison, that I only have that identification, and they purchased my ticket. So, she looks at my ID again, and as she is typing in my name, she says, "That's not a government-issued ID. I smiled and said, "It really is."

I fly into Chicago, O'Hare Field, and since there is not a gate number on my ticket for my connecting flight, I have to go find the departure board. I arrived at 6:14, go to the bathroom, find the departure board, locate my gate, which had already been closed. The flight was scheduled at 6:47 and left on time. Boarding was at 6:17, so I never had a chance.

So, now the reigns slipped. There is no other flight to Jacksonville that day or night. I'm in the United Airlines terminal and don't want to get lost trying to find a different airline because I know I will have to call "somebody" to let them know what's going on. I called the halfway house collect. They won't take the call. (Did you know there are no change machines at O'Hare?) I called my husband and he used his three-way. The halfway house says, "Call the institution." I get cut off about three times because the switchboard keeps transferring me. Finally, with my husband's assistance, I reach one of the lieutenants and give him the number of the payphone I'm on. He's says he'll call me back. I just knew they were going to send the US marshals to come pick me up and I resigned my self to the fact. After playing phone tag for a couple of hours, they tell me to get on the next flight at 6:15 a.m. I spent the night at the airport but that was okay. God is good!

AUTHOR NOTE: Carrie has joined her family in Florida and continues to bless me with her friendship. She now stays in touch by e-mail.

After many years of service, P.O. Box 666 still looks the same. The exterior door hasn't melted or fallen off its hinges. I no longer hesitate when the key is in the lock, but I'll admit to checking things out. There's still a clear view of the mailroom, and I think the temperature is a few degrees warmer than it used to be. Not HOT like you might imagine, but just the right kind of warm, like the love of Jesus. When I reach inside and touch those envelopes, everything seems right. And if I'm ever wondering if this is exactly where I ought to be at this time of my life, all I have to do is think about the letter from a young gang member who was in our group for six months.

Ms. Pischke,
I'm holding on and keeping my head up. My time is flying by. I'm happy to say I have a busy little life. I still go to church and find myself reading my Bible. I got a stamp and thought to tell you I'm doing okay and need you to continue to pray for all of us in here and out there that may be going through things. God bless you and keep on keepin' on. You're going to get a blessing. God's got your back. Love, *Alethea*

PART 2

The Women's Stories

On a bright summer day in 2006, I stood in the parking lot of a busy strip-mall comforting an ex-con named Pamela. She'd called me that morning to say her car was on empty and she was looking for a job, so I left work early to meet her at the gas station. Our second stop was the grocery store. The last twenty in my purse bought a bag of basics; eggs, canned vegetables, hot dogs, a pizza, and fruit snacks for the children of her best friend with whom she was staying.

We hugged there in the glaring sunlight among the cars of other shoppers: two women joined in an unlikely friendship, a union of opposite worlds.

Pamela admitted to a relapse. "Cocaine is my drug of choice," she said, leaning against the side of her car. Her words tumbled out in hurried sentences that ran from one subject to the next. She used alcohol at ten, marijuana at fifteen, and cocaine for the past thirty years. She explained that the problem with drugs is that people like her will do anything to get them. I sensed she was warning me to keep my distance, but I couldn't leave. For the moment, I was all she had, and I felt the need to stay and put more band-aids on her gaping wounds.

Both dangerous and vulnerable, Pamela told me she hated herself for all the things she was and couldn't seem to change. She quoted scripture. Said she heard the call of God, felt it was her duty to prevent this from happening to others, but she didn't know how to start when she couldn't even help herself.

"I made the choices," she explained, "and I knew what was right."

Pamela had traveled hard miles in her forty-plus years. She was raised by a godly family, and then raped by her uncle at the age of twelve. Her older sister took her in and tried to make it right, but Pamela would have none of it. She hit the road, moving from place to place. On the streets she took care of herself in the only way she knew how. Her lifestyle took her to jail, then prison and back to the streets.

She held out her arms to say goodbye and pressed her smooth brown cheek against mine. "I feel like such a failure," she said.

"Don't ever call yourself a failure," I told her. "You're very brave." I couldn't find the words to make her feel better, because I knew my simple act of kindness brought her shame.

—⟋⟍—

CHAPTER 12

Robyn

"Drug and alcohol abuse play a role in the incarceration of 80% of the individuals imprisoned in U.S. jails and prisons."[13]

COLUMBIA UNIVERSITY

My name is Robyn, and I am one of the women of Block 12. I was born in Milwaukee, Wisconsin, to a family that moved approximately every three years. My father was a plant manager for large manufacturing companies, and he was either transferred or he chose to change jobs frequently.

As a child, uncertainty became a way of life for me. Moving meant having the rug pulled out from under my feet and losing my whole life. Painful as that was, it was a familiar feeling. It was what I knew. Relocation was a given. It was just a matter of when. It should not surprise you that I have trouble maintaining long-term relationships.

Moving meant constant change. Everything the other kids were wearing, the slang they used, the music they listened to were all new to me. Assimilation became my way of life, a survival skill that ensured companionship. But I remember the move when I no longer wanted to make this connection, to have friends that I was going to lose anyway. That's when it became easier and made more sense to be alone. That is when my addiction really took hold.

The first time I was offered drugs, I was in Junior High. I was hanging around with a group of girls that had known each other since kindergarten. I was the new girl…again. When they lit up a marijuana pipe and offered it to me, I remembered something my father said to me.

"If someone can't give you a *good* reason for doing something, don't do it."

I asked the girls why I should have some pot and they didn't have an answer, so I said "no." I never did feel like anything but an outsider in that group.

A year or two later, just before my freshman year in high school, we moved from the Midwest to Massachusetts. I was fourteen years old, and I couldn't have been more terrified. We shopped for clothes but didn't really know the east coast styles. The first day of school was devastating. I didn't fit in. In addition, I was a whole year younger than my peers (I was given a test and skipped kindergarten when we moved from Alabama to Tennessee). Now, one year might not seem like a big difference, but I was living in a culture of fifteen-year-olds with the maturity of a fourteen-year-old and, I believe it strongly affected the choices I made.

In my family we knew how to act in public and were always kind and considerate to outsiders. We were not kind to each other. I often wonder if we just took each other for granted, figuring it didn't matter how we treated family members. Talking about our feelings was strictly taboo. My parents overreacted to any sign of emotion, so we knew better than to let our thoughts and feelings show. I believe this is the way my parents were taught growing up, and it was all they knew.

While in Massachusetts, the first group of kids I made friends with were good kids. They were experimenting with alcohol at that time, and I did, too. I remember that I couldn't come up with any reason *not* to try drinking. The days of saying "no" were over for me. Wow! How my perspective changed.

I met a boy I liked, and migrated to another group of kids. They did drugs. I remember the first time I was high on marijuana. I don't know the where or when or with who of that first time. But I do remember that after school (where I must have gotten high), I cleaned my parents' house and did all the chores. When my mom got home, she scolded me for leaving a plate in the sink. I could never do anything right or good enough for her, but this time it didn't hurt so much. As I write these words about my mom, it brings a sick feeling to my stomach, even after all these years, but not that day. When I was high, it just didn't feel like anything. Bingo! From that point forward, I knew what my goal was.

I smoked a quarter ounce of Colombian a week that's twenty-five joints. I drank on weekends and tried any and all drugs that crossed my path: acid, mushrooms, and cocaine. Alcohol and marijuana were the regulars with the rest being recreational. Acid was my favorite recreational drug. It created an altered state of reality that required at least five hours of time away from my parents' house. I believe that's what made it so appealing. The drugs and alcohol became my coping skills. They worked, so I continued to use them. We lived in Massachusetts for two years, then moved back to the Midwest. I was 1,100 miles away from my first love. We had been dating and using drugs together for over a year. I was sixteen, beginning my junior year in high school, and I knew no one. But this move was different. I brought my new coping skills with me.

Drugs were not as easy to find in the Midwest, and they were much more expensive, so alcohol played a bigger part in my life. My first semester at the new school, I earned a 3.75 grade-point average. By the end of second semester I had a 1.5. At the new school, grades were determined by how many classes you skipped and who you hung around with. I had college prep classes and did "A" work but that didn't fly because of the rest of my behaviors.

I graduated and started college at seventeen. Except for a few fleeting moments, drugs did not fit in here. Alcohol was the ticket and lots of it. I earned only three credits the first year of college.

I was kicked out of college, moved home, and worked various jobs. I am fairly intelligent and have good social skills, so I was able to obtain livable wages in the working world. Of course, I chose to work in bars and restaurants and was managing after one year. This was perfect for my addictive nature. I got to spend all of my time with people that partied like me, even while I was working.

I met the father of my son when I was still in high school. He was five years older and much further along in his alcoholism. We began dating after I came home from college. This man was drop-dead gorgeous and a lot of fun. He was everything I was looking for at eighteen.

A year later, I was pregnant. He wanted to get married. This was not a planned pregnancy, and I did not want to compound the problem by getting married. I thought I could take care of the baby and myself, but I didn't think I could take care of all three of us. I broke up with him. My boyfriend was devastated. Every six months he would ask if we could get back together. This was also how often he inquired about his son.

When Jamie was five, his father died in a one-car, alcohol-related accident. Until that time, my son knew his dad as "the guy from the farm." I told him who he was. This disease of alcoholism hurts the best of people.

Jamie is the love of my life. I have never known or felt love like this. During my pregnancy, my doctor, who was also an infertility specialist, asked if I would like to give my child up for adoption to one of the couples he was working with. Both of my sisters also offered to raise my unborn child, but I could not give him up. I knew that I did not have the financial means or the stability that a child deserves, but I had love. He would have my love.

Unfortunately, I also had a pretty serious addiction that had not really reared its ugly head in the way of consequences. I guess you could say I was a functioning alcoholic and addict until Jamie was about five years old. Jamie and I had an apartment. I worked full-time and waited tables one night a week.

One day, my dad came to see me. He asked where I wanted to be in five years. I had never asked myself that question or set any goals. So, I moved home to my parents' house and went back to school at a local technical college. This was the perfect scenario for my addiction. My parents loved Jamie very much, and with live-in babysitters, I could come and go as I pleased. College lasted one year.

I worked full-time as a bookkeeper and tended bar on Sundays. I began dating the owner of the bar. We snorted a lot of cocaine after hours. Then late one night, he introduced me to a better way. He said it was healthier for you. He mixed the cocaine with baking soda and cooked the impurities out of it. You could do an eighth of an ounce and go right to sleep afterward as opposed to laying around for eight hours waiting for your body to slow down. I believed him. After all, I hadn't said "no" to a drug since the ninth grade.

This is when all hell broke loose in my life. The addiction to what I later learned was crack cocaine is like no other. For the next year, my boyfriend and I would do crack for three-day stretches. We only left his house to get more. Then we would sleep for a day, eat for a day, and start smoking again. I am five feet, six inches tall, and I only weighed 102 pounds with boots on. I missed an entire year of Jamie's life getting high at a house just a half-mile from his school. Even now, many years later, I cannot write this without bawling. It feels like my heart is breaking all over again.

One morning, I had a heart attack. We had been smoking for about four days, and my left arm went numb. At first I didn't say anything to my boyfriend. I had a pretty good idea what was wrong and that I would probably die if I kept smoking. I kept smoking. By the grace of God, we were almost out of drugs, and I went to the hospital in time. Addiction is evil. It took precedence over my life. Did I mention I hate this disease?

At the writing of this story, I am 39 years old. I have been through countless treatments prior to and after getting into legal trouble for writing bad checks and stealing money to support my cocaine addiction. Block Twelve is where my addiction took me, but not where my story ends.

Jamie has a "B" average at one of the top colleges in the country, and I am developing a life—a healthy life. I am doing it sober by the grace of God and a twelve-step group. I am doing it one day at a time.

—m—

"Nationwide, more than 57% of women in state prisons and 55% of women in local jails report having been physically and/or sexually abused in the past."[14]

BUREAU OF JUSTICE STATISTICS

CHAPTER 13

Gooch

—⟋⟍—

I am the oldest in a family of five children. My mom worked the night shift, and my dad didn't work at all. At the age of eleven, my biological father raped me repeatedly. I finally got to my feet and ran away. I then called my mom and told her what happened.

My mother is a very private person. She told me it was a lie and hung up the phone. I was devastated. The only other person I could trust was my grandmother, but I felt if I told her she might say the same thing as my mom and then I wouldn't have anyone. From that day on, I never spoke of it.

I had to play the game with my father, trying not to let him catch me. Sometimes he did. Sometimes he didn't. I was labeled the "bad one." No one would listen to me so I closed down.

I was a pretty girl. There was this older boy who wanted to be my boyfriend. I didn't care for him, but he took advantage of me. I was fourteen and ended up pregnant. I wanted to keep my baby, so my mother placed me in a home for unwed mothers. My grandmother came and signed me out and took me home with her. Shortly after I had the baby, my mother came and took me home. My son and I grew up together.

By this time, my father left, and my mom needed help with my siblings. I started stealing to help her financially. Until I was seventeen, I only got caught twice. Both times my mom came and got me. She just told me to be careful. I was getting money from the state, and I helped with the bills. We were doing okay. I went back to school, and she babysat for me. As I continued to steal, I made a name for myself on the streets.

At age eighteen, I met a guy and instantly fell in love. I was thirsty for life. I liked the strokes I was getting. Well, my boyfriend opened up a door of prostitution, forgery, and a lot of other illegal things. I was very good at all I put my mind to and everyone wanted me as their girl.

My boyfriend was so jealous and beat me for stupid reasons. I was miserable, but he wouldn't let me leave. He would threaten my family to get me to come back, and of course, I did. Then he'd beat me silly. I ended up pregnant, and he received a prison sentence. That was my way out, and I took it.

My life changed, and my kids and I were all right. I met another guy, and we got serious. Low and behold, he started to put hands on me, too. I vowed not to tolerate it. I'd had enough, and I left.

I tried weed and didn't like it. I didn't like alcohol either, so I thought, "If I don't care for something, I can stop it."

My best friend asked me, "Did I smoke?"

I told her, "No."

She taught me some things about cocaine. I was hooked within a month.

By trade, I am a certified nursing assistant and dialysis technician. I started calling in sick and had some "no shows." I went from job to job. My cocaine habit was about $500 a day. My family stayed at a distance.

I could no longer cope with having a job, so I joined a forgery ring. I liked to dress well and couldn't see myself doing any and everything for drugs. I believed the whole world was a stage and everybody played a part. I was good at acting by now. I mastered the forgery game and became one of the Number One runners.

My cocaine use increased from $500 to $1,000 a day. I dressed well and stayed high all the time. I could still function after being up for three or four days.

My life came to a standstill when I took someone to the bank and was arrested while waiting for her. She told her life story and everything else.

Truth in sentencing started in January 2000, and the judge threw the book at me. I got ten years—seven in prison and two extended supervision. Wow! I was devastated, so when I got to prison, the psychiatrist was the first person I dropped a slip for. I couldn't accept the amount of time. He gave me enough medication to knock me out. For the first two years, I stayed high and numb.

Some of the people I knew in prison started to say, "Barb, please stop taking so many drugs." One day, I was looking out the window and saw a purple spaceship land on the building we eat in. I freaked. I couldn't leave. I called my mother, and she asked me to please get off the medications.

By this time, my children were grown. I hadn't had a visit for the first five years of my prison term. It was as if I didn't exist. I sat and cried for my family, my kids. No one seemed to care.

I took it on myself to stop taking all my medications. I had been on heavy medication, and it took me almost three weeks. I couldn't sleep or eat. I had sweats, and I was very irritable. I weighed 225 pounds because of the side effects. I was determined.

I looked for help. They have a spiritual channel called TBN that stays on 24 hours a day. I began watching numerous ministers, and I watched them faithfully. I signed up for a Bible study, one-on-one, and I started to really understand our God.

I had been so angry at God that I really didn't believe in him. I've heard God does things for a reason. I never found out that reason, but I do know he allowed me to get this far.

Today, I no longer take. I give and I give from my heart. My life has been hard. Every time I was in an abusive relationship, I found a way out. Don't let anyone abuse you, physically or mentally. Today, we can say "no" and mean it.

The biggest regret I have is all the time I wasted. I could have been anything I put my mind to. The saying, "A mind is a terrible thing to waste," is so true. The worst thing anyone can take from you is your freedom. Believe me! It took me 50 years to realize that. Ain't nothing slick about the lifestyle, the drugs. Nothing is worse than prison.

This prison life has taught me how much I value the little things. It's taught me I am somebody, and God has given me another chance. Where I come from, we had a saying, "Be true to the game and the game will be true to you." Believe me, the only true thing about the "game" is that it will guarantee you a habit, jail, and eventually death.

I'm not ready to die. Today I have God in my life. I want to live and never give up.

"One of the most striking characteristics of incarcerated women is that the proportion who are of racial and ethnic minority background greatly exceeds their representation in the general population."[15]

AMNESTY USA

CHAPTER 14
Pamela

—⟶ɯ⟵—

My name is Pamela and I am from Arkansas. My parents' names are Dorothy and Alonso. My father is deceased. My mother is still living. My mother had seven kids in all. One was stillborn. Two of my brothers are deceased. Currently, there are four living siblings. I have three children and four grandchildren.

I was born and raised in Pankees Addition, a small town near Little Rock. It was a close community where everybody kind of looked out for everybody else. It was back in the days, you know, when you got into trouble, and everyone seemed to "tag" your behind. When you did something wrong, everybody knew it before you'd get back to your house. There'd be three, four, or five chastisements before you'd get home.

I had a pretty good upbringing, you know. My mom and my dad and their kin (grandparents and such), they came from God-fearing families in which we had to get up and go to church every Sunday. We had Sunday school and summer Bible school, too.

We had a good time when we were kids. I remember when we used to go through the woods and dig worms and walk down the road and play, and my father used to take us to work with him. He was like a handyman, and he had all kinds of odd jobs around the neighborhood. He always taught us how to do different things. I remember my father used to comb my hair and plait it and get me dressed up to go to work with him. On those days, he wouldn't take me to school. If we didn't go to school, he would take the time out to teach us to read and teach us math and how to spell. But I think the most important thing about my father, what I loved so much, was he was a God-fearing man. He always told us about God. He taught us to believe and trust in God, just like my grandparents did.

Me and my brothers, we'd bring wood and tote water and help hang the clothes on the clothesline and then bring the clothes in. We wasn't fortunate enough to have an indoor toilet. We had a backdoor toilet, and we bathed in big ol' round tubs and cooked on a big iron stove and everything like that. But it was fun! Sometimes I wish that those days were like today because it was so much fun! And I had my brothers, and I still had my dad, too, and my grandparents who taught me and my younger brother a lot of things. I loved them all so much.

As kids coming up in the country, we was bussed a little ways from where I lived to school. Most of the blacks who went to the school all knew each other because we lived in pretty much the same communities from Mommel to Roland to Natural Steps to Bigelow. We all went to the same high school and elementary school. It wasn't like being in the city of Little Rock where Central High School was going through its changes. But for the most part, we learned to survive and get around different situations.

When I was twelve, my father died. He was only about forty-two. My aunt and uncle, his twin brother, came to the funeral. I was so grieved, I didn't want to stay in Pankees Addition anymore, so my mother sent me to live with them. That was sometime in 1973 or '74. I lived with my aunt and uncle until I was about fourteen, getting ready to turn fifteen. My mother came and got me. I was pregnant with my uncle's child.

At fifteen, after I had my son, Social Services in Arkansas put us in an apartment. I wasn't ready to be a mother, plus I really didn't know anything. I was a country girl. I never had to raise myself, you know. I knew how to get up and clean myself up and do chores and cut wood. I didn't know anything except about being a kid. My son was taken away from me and adopted.

After that, I guess, I strayed away. I could never say that I ever really lacked anything. You know I had lots of discipline at home, lots of love, but I guess somewhere down the line...I don't know. I guess I was the kind of kid that was always curious and wanted to learn about different things.

When I got into the world, as most of us do, I went astray. I went into juvenile when I was like sixteen or seventeen years old after losing my son. I was in trouble. I got into prostitution. I never had a pimp, but I prostituted to take care of myself. I started smoking marijuana when I was like fifteen. I didn't run away from home. I stayed in the community. There was a lot of things going on, you know. I was having sex with older men in the area. That wasn't a good thing, but at the time, I was lost. My father had died. My mother, she was doing something different. I didn't have my son. I was having problems with my grandparents—you know how they say—a disobedient child. I was being disobedient at the time.

As I was going on in my addiction, just from smoking weed, I ran into all kinds of people. I experienced homosexuality. I was into all kinds of things. I was stealing. I was doing everything that I shouldn't have been doing. And the things that I was taught to do, those are the things I neglected.

I went from Arkansas to every state you could imagine. I was pregnant and trying to run away from myself. I went cross-country hitchhiking and met up with a guy in Texas named Derek. Everyone called him Blue Jesus. I never understood why, but anyway he was real good to me. Took me in and took care of me. He was there at the hospital when I had my daughter. He named her Utasha.

I left Tasha (as we called her) with a relative in Pankeys Addition and went back on the road. A trucker picked me up in Arkansas, and I fell asleep. When I woke up, I was in Metropolis, Illinois. I stole some money, and they put me in jail.

Derek came to my rescue. He picked up my daughter in Arkansas and bailed me out of jail. After that, he took me to Chicago where his mother and other family members lived. But they really didn't like me because he came from a family with different values.

They didn't take to me, so what Derek did was take me to his grand-mother's house in Milwaukee. He left me there for a few days and went to find my sister who lived there and let her know I was all right. Then he took my baby and me to my sister Lilly's house and left us there. He would come back periodically and check on us, you know, but his mother was giving him a hard time, so eventually he went back to Chicago. From there he went back to Dallas, I guess. I don't really know because I haven't seen him in twenty-seven years.

When I got to Milwaukee at nineteen, I was wild. My sister and I used to fight like cats and dogs because she was trying to get me back on the right path. She had pretty much helped raised my younger brother Leslie and me. She made sure we had clean clothes when my momma had to work. And when my dad didn't take us with him to work, we had to go by her. I dreaded going by her because I knew she would always have us doing something I didn't want to do, like cleaning and totin' water, and I always wanted to play.

Anyway, when I got to Milwaukee, I got into more prostitution and stealing. It was a lot worse this time because I had graduated from marijuana to cocaine. Now, I didn't know anything about free-basing or crack or anything, because at that time it wasn't called crack. It was free-basing, but I didn't know anything about that. I basically, you know, snorted cocaine and always had all kinds of wild and crazy relationships that always entered into violence or something of that nature.

As time went on, I got into more trouble and more violence and bad relationships and more prostitution and more drugs. Somewhere in 1981 I went into Taycheedah. I was there for about eighteen months or so, got out in 1983, and went and lived up north in Oshkosh. My daughter and I stayed with a young lady I met in Milwaukee who was a dancer. I stayed there for awhile and caught a drug case with the Feds. I went to the Federal joint and was there into 1986. I stayed with the Feds up until about 1995 when I came off paper. I was in and out of the federal joint for dirty urines. I didn't catch another case, but I still was into my addiction.

I can only remember me being clean and sober maybe eighteen months during that time I was dealing with probation and parole with the Feds. I had been in hundreds of different programs. I can't even count all the programs and treatment centers I went through during the whole time of my addictions with the Feds. They had me in every treatment program you could possibly imagine, but my not wanting to change at that time caused me more and more problems. I was more into my addiction.

To go back a little further, before then, me and Tasha was living on Vine Street in Milwaukee. She was still quite young. I guess maybe she was about three years old or so. Social Services came in and took her because I was living a crazy life. I left her in the house one day, and I went down to get some drugs. The social worker happened to be pulling up as I was coming into the house and noticed that I didn't have my baby. After that, they took Tasha and gave her to Lilly. Lilly kept Tasha until she was eleven or twelve—maybe thirteen or fourteen. She was kind of shuffled around.

Then I had my son, Keith, who I wasn't gonna have. I was gonna have an abortion. I have had two abortions and three living children. But my sister talked me into having Keith, and I'm so glad I did because he is a good son. I have wonderful children.

After I was all caught up with the Feds and finished with them, I was pretty much clean. I wasn't really clean, clean, but I wasn't going back and forth to jail. After I finished with the Feds, I think I might have had one or two encounters with goin' to jail off some more humbug stuff. But after I got all that cleared out, I didn't go back to jail, but I was still in my addiction. I didn't work too much. I was doing more hustling than anything, and if I had a job, it didn't last very long because I was too high to get up to go to work or even attend a job or anything like that. As time progressed, I tried to get things together, but it seemed like I was still going on a fast road.

So I went back to Arkansas thinking that I could escape some of the things back in Wisconsin, and I ran into more trouble. It was between 1996 and '97, and it was a tragedy. I was worse into my addiction than ever before. I lost my brother, who was murdered. That was the most devastating day of my life.

I was sick; there was a parasite in my body. I had sores all over me from being in drug-infested houses and smokin' with people. My best friend, Vanessa, was with me at that time. She is still my best friend, and today she is a deacon and youth choir director in her church. She and I went through so many things. I just thank God that I had somebody, like her around me in my life in spite of my addictions. She was my friend then, and she still is today.

During all that time, I had a bad spiritual warfare. I'm still having this warfare with God and me. I feel the fight everyday. Instead of surrendering, I still have my days where I fight and I battle with him. I know that I'm not going to win the fight, but there is something in me that always has to be disobedient.

Through it all, I have to say that God has sustained my life, and I appreciate all the things that He has done for me in spite of my disobedience and in spite of my condition. If it had not been for God, I would not be sitting here today telling you these things.

I'm blessed, and that's the truth. All the things I've been through, I couldn't have come this far without God. Back in Arkansas, a lady hit me in the head with an axe stick and was trying to kill me. If it weren't for the grace of God getting me out of that house, I wouldn't be here today.

I've got a wonderful family. They support me. It's just, I'm hard-headed. And I guess, sometimes you don't appreciate those things that are important to you until you're incarcerated.

This last time, which was in 2003, I was revocated because I had started back to using crack. Before that I was just selling crack but after awhile, I started using. And so that led me back into the system once again. I was only a few months away from getting off of probation and I blew it. I went to the County Jail and was revoked, and during the time that I was revoked, the state brought charges against me for possession, for selling cocaine.

I went to Taycheedah for about eighteen months. I got out January 2006. I thank God for all that he has done for me because, truly, I could have gotten much more time. I got two years plus five years on paper—seven in all.

I can't begin to tell you how grateful I am for all the opportunities and chances I've gotten 'cause I know that I've had chances in life that only God could have given me through other people, especially my family and my two friends, Vanessa and Diedre. They have stuck by me through my addiction and all the ups and downs of my life. That is a blessing. God always puts the right people in your life at the right time and for the right reasons.

It is my hope that my story can help somebody. Whoever is out there, if they feel they are alone and they're by themselves in their addiction and they've been molested and they've been mistreated and stepped over and done wrong to, I just want them to know, hey, I've been there too. But I know that there is a God, and he always makes a way.

Yeah, I know some people say, "I know there's a God, but how come he lets this happen or that happen?" But sometimes we have to look at ourselves, too. Some things, we don't have any control over. But the things that we have control over, those are the things that we have to take the initiative to take hold of and make a difference and make changes.

Change is hard, but change is good. It's uncomfortable, but once you get that uncomfortable period away from your life and get the comfortable period in your life, that's the best thing. God is always there no matter what's going on, no matter how you may be feeling, no matter how you think things may be. And there is no condition in your life that God cannot change. No matter what people say, no matter what people do, no matter how they talk about you and put down, or say you'll never be anybody, you'll never amount to anything, remember God says, "Through Christ, all things are possible."

When God says, "Forgive," that's the best thing that you can do. When you forgive and let go, you have released that which is a monster or a demon inside of you. Now what other people do with that, that's on them. But when you let it go and you let your insides be healed by God, it's gonna be a good healing process for you. It ain't gonna be easy because bitterness is like a germ or a disease. You can't get rid of it unless you take the right medication. Certain things happen to people in their lives, and they blame God for it and they have a bitterness of holding on to things. In order to heal properly, you have to let go.

I understand that letting go doesn't always mean that you're gonna forget about it, but in order to let go of it you have to release it, and some parts you do have to forget. I'm not sayin' it's gonna be totally wiped out. You have to allow whatever you went through to be a process, to get through it, because if you hold on to it and you let it fester inside, it'll grow and grow.

It's just like cancer. It'll eat you up and eat you up and you'll become bitter and hostile and violent and rebellious. And no one can get in to help you, not even God, because there's nothing that he can do with a hardened spirit. Just like Pharaoh. He hardened his heart, and there was no way God could even get in to make any kind of changes. In order to make changes in your life, you have to be able to have a soft heart. You have to humble yourself so that God can get in to mend whatever it is that's hurting, that's cut up, that's broken. And you know, he can't get in there and heal those things if you don't allow him to.

For those of you who are out there struggling, who feel like they don't have any chance or no way to get out of their situation, believe in God and trust in God and I guarantee you, he'll make a way. And with that, God bless!

—m—

"Nearly one in three women in state prisons reported committing their offense to support a drug addiction."[16]

BUREAU OF JUSTICE STATISTICS

CHAPTER 15
Diane

—⚬—

My name is Diane. My life trials started at the age of thirty-four. My father died in 1984, and prior to that I always held down a job. I graduated from high school in 1974 and went on to get an associate's degree in Early Childhood Education. I always wanted one child of my own and gave birth to a baby girl in 1978.

I continued to work but became involved with a known drug dealer I met at a bar. As time went on, I realized this man liked me more and more and in my mind, I believed partying and doing drugs with him was just fine for me. I knew he had a wife, but she was aware of his life style, and I was okay with that, too. He had a good job and used his money wisely.

This man started coming by my apartment on a nightly basis, and he would bring me dope every time. I had enough to get high all day and all night, if I wanted to, and I did. At this time, my daughter was four years old. I had to get her ready for school and myself ready for work. The man started spending the night, and eventually his wife found out about me.

As years passed, my drug habit became my life. My daughter was never home and that gave me time to indulge in my drug behavior. My addiction became so bad I lost my job for calling in sick and not being able to function at work because I was thinking about getting high.

I realized I had to do something because I could not take care of my apartment and living expenses. I realized I had to get rid of the problem and thought that meant the man. So I did that, thinking I would be all right. Not! I took what money I had and bought more drugs.

I couldn't call him for drugs anymore. I lost my apartment and had to move back with my parents. They knew I had a drug problem, but I was in denial. They encouraged me to get help. I agreed to that and went into rehab. I completed the program and stayed clean for a while. I found a job and ran into some people who got high and started hanging out with them after work. When my parents found out, they were very upset.

After a time, I lost that job. I couldn't work because of the hangovers and thinking about getting high. I went back into treatment and completed another program. I was still living with my parents. My father became ill. I got a third-shift job, at St. Mary's Hospital and cared for him during the day. Well, my father died, and I couldn't handle that, so I started getting high again and lost my job because of the drugs.

Things got so bad between my mother and me, I had to move from her house. I called a guy I dated when I was seventeen and told him I had problems at home. He sent a cab for me, and eventually I moved in with him. My daughter, who was seven, moved with me.

Well, James didn't know that I did crack cocaine. He brought some home and asked me to cook it for him. He knew I got high in the past but thought I was clean for some years now. He told me the cocaine was for someone else, but it was for him. I knew he snorted, but I didn't know he smoked. That incident opened the door for me to get high again.

James had a very good job and was able to support me. I told him I wanted to work and get my life back on track. He just wanted me to stay home, so I did. In my idle time I went to the mall not far from my house and started stealing things. I wanted to get high and couldn't take the household money because James would find out. I ran into a drug dealer, and she started meeting me there. Eventually, I caught a case while James was at work. That was my first charge ever—forgery/credit card. I went to jail and was released on bond. My behavior continued, and I was sentenced to probation. The year was 1989. I continued to steal, and my probation was revoked. I went to Taycheedah Correctional Institution. I was there two weeks and was transferred to a work release camp. I did six months and received a grant to go home.

I stayed straight for a while because I was on parole and had to report to my agent. My old behavior returned. I stopped seeing my agent and was stealing every day. I caught another case, went to jail, and my agent gave me an alternative, a halfway house. The judge gave me probation with a stayed sentence if I did my time at a Huber facility. I was there one day and left. I got charged with a felony escape. I was caught stealing and went back to prison for nine months.

The second time in prison didn't change my attitude. I came out and started stealing again. I found a job. My addiction was no longer drugs, but stealing. My behavior continued, and I kept catching cases. The judge gave me three years. I served two and was released in 1999. I had one year of parole left. I completed that and entered a program for employment training for individuals who needed a second chance in life. The program lasted four months, and I was hired full-time the same year.

The job required me to have a driver's license and car. I got both the year of 2001. I was blessed, doing all the right things, and I had a lady who encouraged me and supported me spiritually and mentally. I worked the job for two-and-a-half years. I became comfortable and thought I had myself together.

I decided to dip and dab, and finally, I was getting high all over again. The job and the program closed down, so I received unemployment. I had a hard time finding work because of my criminal record. In 2002 I found a job as an administrator for a daycare center. I had my degree in early childhood education and remained there until the center was closed. I started stealing a little, and it became a greater habit, once again. By 2002, my stealing habit became so powerful I could not control it. I caught another case and served a year in Huber.

After that, I ran into the guy I knew at seventeen. He had been in prison for twelve years. We started talking, going to church, and doing the right thing. I gave myself to the Lord. His brother and sister-in-law were ministers. We hung out together, and even though I couldn't find work, I prayed daily, and the Lord kept my spirits with Him. I wasn't stealing.

We moved in together, but that was my worst mistake. I thought he was going to take care of me. Unfortunately, he had problems with his family, and I was unhappy. I lived with a girlfriend for about a month and started stealing again. I went back to him for exactly one week. I went to church one Sunday morning, and I surrendered to God. After church, I went stealing. Guess what? I was caught in April of 2006 and I have been in prison ever since.

Today, I realize "doing time" has got to be about Diane and no one else. I have been lonely in all areas of my life. All my life I have been looking for compassion, love, respect, prosperity, kindness, and acceptance from the ones I loved. I was looking for these things in my addictions, and I was bringing myself down more and more.

I know now only God can deliver and heal me. All I have to do is be obedient and faithful. I must let Him lead my life because I seem to fail at everything I do. I look at myself today, and I will not let past failures haunt me or lead me astray. I will look to God and pray for everything I need. I know He will provide for me. I will continue to grow in my faith and stay around positive people. I will serve the Lord with all I have and that means giving up everything to Him. I know my future will be bright and joyful.

Just as winter turns to spring, my life is changing seasons. Today, when the forecast is gloomy, I will remember God has plans for me. Instead of praying for a change in my circumstances, I will pray for a change in my heart.

—m—

"If all inmates who needed treatment and aftercare received such services, the nation would break even in a year if just over 10 percent remained substance and crime-free and employed."[17]

THE NATIONAL CENTER ON ADDICTION AND SUBSTANCE ABUSE

CHAPTER 16

Tammie

—〜〜—

They say in order to recover and heal people must forgive themselves. To do that, we must face the demons from the past that kept us in our addiction and the things we did while we were in that addiction.

I personally have come a long way in my recovery, which for me has been a very, very, long and slow process. Process is the key word here. First and foremost, I have admitted (albeit thirteen years ago) I was powerless over drugs, and my life had become unmanageable. Just admitting this was half the battle. The other half is, for all intents and purposes, the *rest of my life*! That's the process.

I have come to terms with my current situation: prison and what led me here. However, I cannot seem to forgive myself for the things I've done, people I've hurt, and situations I've created. That keeps me from healing and recovering.

Let me give you a bit of background so some of what I've said makes sense. You know the saying, "You can't judge a book by its cover." That's where I'm going with this story.

My name is Tammie, and I am 45 years old. I was born in 1960 and grew up in a predominantly white, upper-middle-class neighborhood in Kenosha, Wisconsin. Kenosha is largely a blue-collar city on the shores of Lake Michigan half way between Chicago, Illinois, and Milwaukee, Wisconsin.

There was really no one in my family who smoked cigarettes, abused alcohol, or did any drug—legal or illegal. Nothing. There was no incest, no beatings, and no sexual molestation going on.

It was all very boring, very "That 70's Show," and very typically white. I never got in trouble with the law. I was a fat kid who was teased, a follower, never a leader. I was a brat and argued with my parents, mostly my mother, all the time.

I grew up in the same house while attending elementary school, junior high, and high school, even college. Boring!

I always wanted to fit in but never felt as if I did. I was that fat kid that no one wanted to hang around with, the last one picked for dodge-ball games on the playground.

By the time junior high rolled around, when I was twelve or thirteen, I started smoking cigarettes to be cool and fit in. I also started drinking beer and smoking pot. I really felt cool then. I was still fat and I felt ugly. In high school I became active in sports playing softball and attending all the sporting events. I really didn't smoke or drink too heavily, just enough for fun. Then there were pills. Speed mostly, black Cadillacs, white cross, pink hearts, and others.

By the time I graduated from high school in 1978, I was already getting into bars. I was seventeen, the drinking age was eighteen but no one ever got carded. Next came college, my first boyfriend, and a fake college I.D. that gave my age as twenty-one. That allowed me to drink in Wisconsin and Illinois.

I went through my college years, all five of them, stoned or hung over. I accumulated enough credits to be considered a senior and then dropped out. My parents moved to California that same year (1983). I didn't go with them. I got my first apartment and my very first taste of freedom. I was twenty-two years old and thought I had the world by the ass.

My mother passed away in 1986. I was twenty-five years old. That's when I started my twenty-year affair with a drug I loved more than life itself—cocaine. I was also downing Xanax and painkillers (Percocet, Vicodin, and Oxycontin) at an alarming rate. I was eating enough of those pills in amounts that could have killed me even without the cocaine. I added heroin to the mix nineteen years later on my 43rd birthday.

To graduate to heroin was insane! I did not see it coming. I started having blackouts. I don't remember my 43rd birthday or the following two weeks.

I was blacking out days and weeks at a time. I did not remember going to work, getting behind the wheel of a car, or even where I put my lit cigarette. I drove places day and night. It didn't matter where. I will never, ever know. It is only by the grace of God that I didn't hurt or kill anyone.

It's funny, but I remember every single "first." The first time I smoked pot, the first time I snorted a line of coke, the first time I smoked it and shot it, and the first time I snorted heroin. I remember crying out to God so hard, I couldn't catch my breath. I cried for some kind of relief, for help. Shortly after discovering heroin and passing the point of no return, I distinctly remember saying "I'm doing as much and as many drugs as I can until I die. I don't care anymore."

Well, that statement never came true. There was a sort of divine intervention—the law! I was arrested and charged with delivery of cocaine, my very first time in trouble. I received a sentence of sixty days Huber (work release, I had a job) and four years probation. I served my sixty days, got out and found myself back in jail 48 hours later. This time I was in a 6 x 8 foot nasty cell with my head in a stainless steel bowl puking my guts out.

I had smoked crack, downed Xanax, and drunk alcohol—enough to choke a horse. The neighbors had to call 911 because I was in the hallway vomiting and screaming something like, "They won't let me in my apartment." I don't know who "they" were, but there was no one present when I was whisked away to the emergency room. I had overdosed.

I "came to" three days later in the Kenosha County Jail. I felt like sh*t and still had head spins. The best part, I caught another felony case, this time for possession of cocaine. Go figure! That was January 15, 2005. I had only been out for two days. I spent twelve months incarcerated—four of those were in an intense drug treatment program. By October of 2005 I was free on a leg monitor, but free.

Six weeks on the ankle monitor was a breeze, however, less than 48 hours later, I was right back at it. *Right back at it!* I didn't learn a thing. Two weeks after getting off the ankle bracelet, I was finally "fitting in!" That is, fitting into my jailhouse blues and oranges, not to mention my prison greens. I wore those until July of 2008.

All those years of doing drugs did nothing but mess me up. I never finished college. I never learned how to deal with any situation, from a simple argument with someone to getting my heart broken. I have used drugs to cover up EVERYTHING. I have stuffed emotions so far down that I know for a fact I need to be clean and sober, behind razor wire to learn how to deal with situations.

I used drugs when I was sad, hurt, angry, happy, or "normal." I used drugs to celebrate holidays, birthdays, and anniversaries. I used drugs to celebrate the sun, the moon, clouds in the sky, rain falling, daytime, nighttime. I was a hot mess.

I never talked to anyone about how I really, truly felt. I did not like myself. As a matter of fact, I hated myself. (I'm still working on that one). I felt I was ugly, fat, and not good enough for a nice guy or anyone else to want to be with me. I thought if I just remained high, I wouldn't have to feel any emotion. I did not want my feelings hurt. I did not want to experience the hurt and sadness when my mother and father passed away. I did not want to feel the pain of my self-hatred. I did not want to feel anything at all...EVER. I was a loser going nowhere, no kids, no husband, not even a boyfriend. Just drugs, drugs, and more drugs.

My mother was a beautiful, wonderful woman who found it hard to open up and express her true feelings and emotions. She never even talked to me about sex. So reaching out to someone does not come easily to me. It is only after two years of confined drug treatment, intensive out-patient treatment, and mandatory "relapse" groups that I am starting to finally get out whatever it is I have been stuffing all those years.

I have lots of work and bridges to build. My sister hasn't spoken to me more than once in the past two years. I don't receive cards, letters, pictures, or visits from my family. My brother, who lives in California, allows me to call. I don't blame them. I have lied, cheated, stolen, and manipulated everyone and every situation in some way shape or form, all this because I was selfish and self-centered. I wanted what I wanted when I wanted it. The "what" I am speaking of is drugs.

I have to forgive myself or I will never make it—never. I'm scared. I'm scared as hell. I can admit my wrongs but I can't forgive. I don't quite know how. All this because I didn't talk about how I really felt inside. But guess what? It's not so hard. What's hard is spending your whole life high on drugs.

The next thing you know it's twenty-five, thirty, thirty-five years later, and you wonder what happened.

Do what you gotta do. Talk to whomever you need to and last, but not least pray. Pray. Pray. Pray. The big guy upstairs is open twenty-four/seven, and He'll never let you down. He won't close a door without opening a window. That's a promise.

I know I'm in prison; however, nothing, and I repeat nothing, compares or comes anywhere close to the prison I made for myself by choosing drugs. You might think, because I'm in prison, that I have failed. I have not! I will only fail if I do not pick myself up, learn from my mistakes, and move forward...*with the strength of a lion and the will of an ant.*

I pray for God to take the taste out of my mouth and most of all, the desire out of my mind. I think I'll be all right. I pray for strength and patience and tolerance every day. You've got to want it. And you know what? It works. It just takes time. I have lots of that.

"After parental incarceration, a child whose father is imprisoned usually lives with the mother, while the child of an incarcerated mother is much more likely to live with grandparents, other relatives, or to be placed with foster care agencies." [18]

NATIONAL COUNCIL ON CRIME AND DELINQUENCY

CHAPTER 17
Michelle

—m—

y name is Michelle. I was born and raised in Wisconsin by two loving, supportive parents. I had a good childhood and wanted for nothing. As I look back on my life, I would have never thought I would be in prison at the age of thirty-seven facing the loss of my three beautiful children.

My troubles started back in my early twenties. I became involved with the man who would affect my life for many years to come. Joe was his name, and he was the father of my two sons, Jordan and Joe, Jr. When I first became pregnant, in 1993, Joe got in trouble for violating his parole and went to prison for three years. I felt abandoned because I had to bring a child into the world alone.

I visited Joe as much as I could, but the separation took its toll on our relationship. I was into having the baby and raising my child. He didn't support me, so I wanted to separate myself from him. I moved in to my own place with my new baby, Jordan, who was born in 1994.

When Jordan was one, I met a man named Robert who was much older than I was. He treated us very well. He moved in with us, and I got pregnant again. Things started to change when I discovered he had a severe problem with drugs. He kept on promising he would get help. I wanted to believe him. I wanted a good life for my children and me.

He put me in danger. People were always showing up looking for him and demanding money for his debts. Robert said tomorrow he would get help. Tomorrow never came. I had enough. I had to protect my son and unborn baby. I told him to leave. He moved to Minnesota and continued with the self-destruction. Drugs were all that mattered to him.

There I was, alone again, and about to have another baby. In 1996, I had a little girl and named her Melody. I had my hands full with a two-year-old and a baby, but I was determined to raise my children.

I found out Joe was out of prison. I decided to get in touch with his family. When I called, he was there. We talked and decided to give it another try. It was like we were never apart. He moved in with us and treated Melody like he was her father. It started out too good to be true.

Eventually, things went down-hill. Joe always wanted to go to Milwaukee. He'd promise to spend time with us, but it never worked out like that. His idea of spending time with us consisted of going to his mom's house. He would leave us with his mom, and he would go upstairs. He'd come down all sweaty and acting funny. It finally came out that he was up there getting high.

I put up with it, and we were in danger again. He owed drug dealers, and they came around demanding money. I told him to make a choice: either come home with us and be a man, or stay in Milwaukee and continue the life he was living. He chose to stay in Milwaukee. Drugs were more important.

I had two children and another one on the way. I couldn't keep doing this and having babies without a father to be there for them. I didn't hear from Joe for about two weeks, didn't know if he was dead or alive. I found out he was in jail with new charges. Robbery landed him in prison with an eight-year sentence. In January of 1997, Joe Jr. was born. I decided this would be my last baby. I couldn't keep having babies and expecting different results.

I loved Joe and stood beside him, always going to visit with the kids. Sometimes we drove two hours one-way to see him. Wherever the system took Joe—Waupun, Fox Lake, or Kettle Morraine—we were there. In 1998 we got married. Life as a prison wife was the closest I could get to him, but the years passed and I drifted away. It destroyed everything we had. We blamed each other.

I became extremely angry with Joe because he wasn't there for us. I had to raise our children alone, and I felt abandoned again. Being in prison was getting to him and he took it out on me. I took the verbal abuse every day when he called home. He didn't trust me. After years of going to visit him, I

just was so tired of his crap. I was sick and tired. He changed and didn't realize what I had to go through. He was the only one that mattered and that just
wasn't enough for our children and me.

I became involved with a male friend whom I had always been in touch
with. It was someone to talk to. We started using drugs together. I just started
with weed. One day, I explored further and started smoking primos; that's
weed laced with cocaine in a joint. It gave me a stronger high. To be honest, I don't know why I started using drugs. I believe it made me think I could
escape from my problems with Joe, Sr., and dealing with the stress of raising
three children alone.

Eventually, I went to smoking cocaine alone because it was so hard to
get weed. Once I tried it, I only smoked crack. My behaviors changed. My
thinking changed. I shut Joe out completely. I guess I didn't want him to know
what I was doing. I tried to hide it, but eventually I shut down. I stopped using
for a while because I had my children to take care of, but my friend came
around and I started again. I was too weak to turn him down.

When I fell behind with my bills, my family backed me up. In 2000 I had
an incident with the law. They referred me to Human Services and petitioned
for protective services for my children for one year. I didn't object because
I knew things were out of control and I had been making poor decisions.
The services would benefit my children. I hid my drug problem initially. They
suspected I was using, so I cleaned myself up for the children because they
needed a clean mom.

I started using again. I ran out of options to pay for my drugs and to
manipulate money from my family. I became greedy and didn't care about the
outcome. Being on drugs made me think I could do anything and never get
caught. I continued this way, and my children were placed in foster care.
I was devastated. My little girl was crying, "I don't want to go." My sons
seemed okay, but they didn't know what was happening. There was a warrant
for my arrest, but they didn't handcuff me in front of the children. The children
were six, four, and three years old, at the time.

Within hours, I was released from jail. My parents bailed me out. I went
home to an empty apartment. The silence was deadly. It was days before I
knew where the children were. Finally, I was able to see them. We cried. They
wanted to go home with me but, of course, that was not possible. It was hard

for me to accept. I only had myself to blame.

I left my apartment. My children were gone, and I felt I had nothing left. Everything was gone and I didn't know how to get it back. Everything was out of control. As I continued to use, I believed everyone was against me and I became desperate. I also believed using marijuana and cocaine would help me cope.

It was then that everything I did was coming back on me. In my drug use, I started committing charges that I am now revoked for. The day after the children were removed from my care, I was called to the police station for charges of forgery. I had found a checkbook months before and wrote out eight checks. At the time, I did not care about the damage I was causing to the stranger whose identity I stole. I bought clothes, toys, anything I needed. I also cashed the checks for amounts over the purchase to buy drugs. It was like Christmas, and for that day, it made my children happy.

I had done a selfish thing to fulfill a selfish need. I was trying to satisfy the hunger I had for cocaine without cheating or manipulating my family. I was not hearing what social services said. I only believed they wanted my children and that I would never get them back.

Most of all, I hated myself. I was in debt with no place to go. I left in a rented car, not knowing where I would go. I moved in with my sister-in-law in Milwaukee. I had problems with her, so I headed south to Rockford to see a friend. On the way, I got stopped. The police were looking for me. I had not returned the car. I knew it was wrong, but I was lying to myself.

I was arrested and released the next morning on a $10,000 signature bond. My friend tried to help me, but I was unwilling to see I had a drug problem. I called my family and went to stay in Rockford. I knew I had to get myself together. A month later, I went too far. I took about thirty pills. I felt helpless. I called my social worker. The authorities took me to the emergency room and pumped my stomach. Then I was transferred to Milwaukee Psychiatric Hospital for evaluation. I was there for three days. I was never so sick in my life. After that, I went to treatment for thirty days. Once released, I went to stay at a homeless shelter.

I was waiting to be sentenced for my two pending charges when I was caught shoplifting and was arrested. I had been out on bail from the previous

$10,000 signature bond. I was in twenty days before my parents co-signed another bond. They wanted to teach me a lesson. Once released, they insisted I stay with them so my dad could watch me.

I was sentenced to seven years' probation. I wasn't assigned a P.O. (probation officer) for 30 days, so I took it upon myself to move out of my family's home. When I finally reported, I knew I was dirty (urine test) and wanted to get out of the agent's office as fast as I could, so I told her I was employed and signed a wage assignment. My P.O. verified and found out I was lying. She called me to report to jail for three days. I never showed. My father encouraged me to turn myself in. I was dirty, so I ended up in Chatham House. This was my chance to get it together, and I did. I went to a four-month program run by probation and parole. They allowed me to see my children once a week and even transported me to the foster home which was forty minutes away.

After four months, I moved into a one-bedroom apartment. A week later, my daughter was returned to my custody because she was having problems and was hard to control. She had an episode where she stripped all her clothes off, screamed uncontrollably, and threw things at anyone who tried to approach her. The police were called, and when they entered the room, she ran to me. She thought they were trying to take me away. I had them take us to the hospital to evaluate her. She was admitted to the children's unit, and it was discovered she had been sexually assaulted. I reported the information to Racine Social Services. She received help through a hospital program for children who have been assaulted.

I blamed myself for a long time and still do. If I hadn't been using drugs, my children would not have been in foster care, and this would never have happened to my daughter.

In June of 2003, Jordan and Joe, Jr., came home. We moved into a new apartment. Each child had a bedroom, and we had a big back yard. I stayed clean for two years. I struggled with my life. My youngest son was diagnosed with severe cognitive delays, ADHD, and bi-polar disorder. I was taking care of my three children and happy. Joe, Sr., and I were still together, as much as we could be, considering our situation. His release date of June 2004 was getting closer. But the closer it came, the more scared I felt. I wanted him to be a father to our children and the husband I never had. My biggest fear was that he would let the kids down.

My son, Joe, liked to play outside. The man next door was always out playing ball with his son. He would talk to Joe. I had always told my children to stay away from strangers, but one day, I had a chance to meet him and found out he was okay. Joe, Jr., became very attached to this man because he spent time with him. That was something his dad never did.

I made a big mistake and became involved with the neighbor. I told him I was married and my husband would be getting out soon. The more time I spent with him, the closer I felt. He made points with me because he was good to the children and gave me the attention I had never received from Joe. I was no longer excited that he was coming home. I hid my involvement. I felt bad that I had betrayed my husband.

I had to tell Joe, but I couldn't leave him. The kids and I had waited eight years for him to come home. I stopped answering the phone when Joe called. I didn't pick him up when he was released. I realized I wanted to hurt him before he hurt me again.

Joe came home, and I told him the truth. He handled it better than I thought. He told me he loved me, and we could work through it. He didn't want us to live there any more and gave me a choice. Either I stayed or I could come with him to Milwaukee. My agent didn't want me with Joe and ordered me not to stay with him. She felt something wasn't right with me and told me to take myself away from it.

She was right. I had been getting high with the neighbor man, and I hid it from everyone: my family, my agent, my counselors, my children, and my husband. I was so ashamed of relapsing after almost two years. I hated myself.

Joe rented a U-Haul and moved me out of my apartment. We moved in with his family and that was against my probation. I was scared. He hit me when he first got home. He told me he was mad and could have killed me and gone back to prison. I went with him and didn't say anything.

My agent called and told me to come to her office or she would lock me up. I went. She told me I could move to Milwaukee but needed to do it right: find a place, doctors, a school for the kids. I was so excited to tell Joe. He had to stay in Milwaukee because he was on the bracelet.

When I arrived home, he was acting funny. He took me in the bedroom and said he had something to tell me. He informed me he had been getting high in prison. He pulled out a pipe.

I was so angry. I lost it. I said, "What the hell are you doing? I'm out of here."

He said, "You're leaving me?"

I asked him, "How can you do this to your kids who have waited all their lives?"

That night, he left to get his fix, stole $1200 worth of dope from his friend who was a dealer, leaving me to pay his debt and putting us in danger again. When Joe Jr., woke up the next day, he was devastated. He said, "Where's my dad?"

I told him, "Honey, I don't know."

With tears in his eyes, he punched the door and said, "He promised he wouldn't leave."

I packed up and went back to Racine. The landlord had changed the locks. We no longer had a home. I went to my friend. He and his family took us in. Within a week, Joe was locked up. He expected me to be there for him, but I couldn't do it any more.

I relapsed again, being around my friend and all the drugs. My P.O. called to see me. I went in and dropped dirty urine. She locked me up and put the kids in foster care.

I went back to jail from July 2004 to January 2005. I successfully completed an AODA program, which I desperately needed. On release, I was ordered to go to a Homeward Bound shelter in Racine. I could talk to my kids on the phone but was not allowed to see them, and that was very hard for me. I stayed at the shelter for one day and went back to see my friend's mother, which was a big mistake.

I was on the run for 18 days, using drugs and leaving everything behind. I asked myself why I continued to do these things and hurt the people I love. I had enough. I didn't want to use drugs any more. I wanted my life back with my children because they deserved better. The last time I had talked to them they asked me, "Mommy, where do you sleep?" I called 911 and turned myself in.

I was revocated from Racine County for violating my probation, dirty urine, having contact with people I was ordered not to see, not reporting to my agent, and missing court. I went back to court and was sentenced to five years in prison and five years extended supervision. I received 429 days credit for time served, and my release date as I write this is April of 2009.

Going to prison was something I earned. No one did it for me. But that wasn't the hardest part. Losing my children was the worst. I haven't seen them since July 1, 2004, and haven't talked to them since April 20, 2005. I am only allowed to have contact by writing to them. Racine County feels it is in their best interest that I don't talk to them because their behavior becomes uncontrollable afterwards. My family calls the children every week and visits them.

I have been petitioned to have my rights terminated as their mother. I will be incarcerated for the next 32 months. They need stability in their lives, and I can't provide it. I am going to trial to fight to keep my rights as their parent. I only want what's best. I want them to be happy. I am torn over what to do. I don't want my children to think I just gave them up. I want them to grow up happy. I talk to the foster mother regularly. She lets me know how they are doing. She loves them, and they are well cared for. She told me she won't let them forget me, she won't let them forget how much I love them, and whatever happens, I will always be their mom.

Being in prison has been an eye-opener for me. For the first time in my life, I have been able to step up and take responsibility for my actions. When I first came here, I was angry at everyone else and blamed them for using drugs and making my life this way. Now I realize that I, Michelle, did this and can blame no one but myself. I can't blame Joe. I made the choices that took me away from my family and friends. For the first time, I am ready to change—for real.

I have a lot of hurt as a result of the separation from my children. I brought it on myself, and I will have to pay for my choices the rest of my life. When I get out, I want to make changes and be a better person for the community and my family. I plan to focus on myself and do what my agent expects of me. I want to live an honest life the way my family raised me. I want to make my parents proud. Living right is all they want from me. They are in their sixties and won't be around much longer. I want to cherish every moment I have left with them.

I put faith in God that he has a plan to be with my children. It may not be the plan I want. I do believe in God as my Savior, and I know that everything happens for a reason. I pray every day and keep faith. It gives me hope for the future. I am thirty-seven years old. I have time for a fresh start, and it begins with being drug-free and learning everything I can in here. It all starts here, and I can use it on the other side of the door.

I believe I have what it takes to learn this lesson. I am learning every day. I am thankful for every day I wake up to opportunities for another chance. I will continue to learn from my past and hope to someday help others as I have been helped.

That is my story. Learn from my mistakes. Prison has given me a lot of time to evaluate myself and find out what I need to change. It started the day I entered the Taycheedah Correctional Institution grounds and will continue for the rest of my life. I want to be a better mother, daughter, and a friend to others. God has blessed me and I am thankful. I needed to come to prison. I needed to change.

The end is a new beginning.

—ᴍ—

"Over three million children witness domestic violence each year." [19]

WOMEN IN PRISON PROJECT

CHAPTER 18
Star

—ɯ—

I am the second oldest of eight children and the first daughter. The first person a child should learn to love and trust is her mother, or so you would think. I believe love and trust are learned behaviors and should come first from your mother, a woman who carried you for nine months. But these two words were not part of my upbringing or vocabulary, and the absence of love and trust scarred me for life, etching a pattern of hatred into my heart.

My parents divorced when I was seven. Our family was quite dysfunctional, father an alcoholic, mother a drug addict. They fought constantly and I was, more or less, a daddy's girl. For some reason, my mother hated all of her girls. I tried to shield the others from her madness the best I could, but I wasn't always successful. My little sister once said she was cold, and I saw her placed on a space heater. The grill marks remain on her skin to this day. When I was eight, I witnessed my youngest sister's death. My mother threw her into metal bunk beds because she was crying. It busted her little head open. It seems it took the rescue squad forever before they came. She needed them quickly. She was going on two years old. I'm still terrified of rescue squads.

The death certificate said she was also dehydrated. I wasn't able to sneak her no water that day as I normally would. My mom would hear the water running and start ranting and raving at me. I often got water out of the back of the toilet—it didn't hurt any of us. That day I truly began to hate with a vengeance. I promised myself that no one would ever hurt one of my siblings again, and when I was older, I would kill the person responsible for my loss.

My little sister's favorite song, the one she used to rock to, was "Chain Gang" by Sam Cooke. To this day, that song makes me cry. The sister next to me grew up believing she was responsible for our sister's death. She didn't tell me this until many years later. I was mad at the world and angry with God because no one cared except me.

I had a little brother who was given away at three days old. We were told it was because he didn't like our mother. A child that age don't know nothin' about their mother. I grew up vowing to protect my babies (my siblings).

I was raped when I was ten years old by my mother's boyfriend. When I told her, I was stripped naked and beaten with an extension cord. The boyfriend held my feet, and my big brother held my arms. Every man my mother ever had raped me. I just hoped none of my sisters would have to go through the same pain.

For the next couple of years, I was taken from psychiatrist to psychiatrist, and they all told me I hated my mother. Hell, I knew that and made no secret of it. Nightmares became an everyday part of my life. My sister that died invaded my sleep, wanting to know why I didn't protect her. I still wrestle with that same question.

I found a gun and tried to kill my mother, but couldn't. She sent me away to a girls' school. When I came back home, her boyfriends still had their way with me. She went to prison for forgery and child abuse. That was a happy moment.

My siblings and I were separated. I kept running away. At fourteen I ran away from the girls' school. I hooked up with these dudes who told my friend (someone who ran with me) that we were going to work. I was so happy. I was going to be able to help my brothers and sisters out. We went stealing so we could eat. Each of us had a mission when we went into a store. Anyway, little did I know the work they talked about was selling our bodies.

The guys bought us nice clothes, and we went to Chicago. One day, the main whore said we weren't gonna work but were going to "kick it." That night we made no money. The pimp came to pick us up and found out. We were beaten with clothes hangers all about the body. I broke out the bathroom window and left. On my own in Chicago, I slept in a park and ate out of garbage cans. I knew no one. I started stealing and hooking for myself.

I met my first husband when I was sixteen. At first, he treated me like a queen. I heard he had several women, but I never cared. Right before my seventeenth birthday, he snapped. He drugged me and tied me down, then stuck a mini-bat lined with razor blades in my vagina. His grandmother found me, and I was taken to a hospital. There I was told I would never be able to bear children because of the extensive damage to my organs.

My husband got two years in prison. I was damaged goods and figured no one would want me. When he got out, I went back to him like a damn fool. He locked me in the house. We had bars on the doors and windows. We had no phone. I wasn't allowed out alone. I had one friend who could come over, but she was a prisoner in his madness, too.

He brought his women to our house, put them in our bed, and force us to have sex with each other. He also brought men and forced me to have them or take a beating. My husband went to California with his sister for two weeks. My friend got a hacksaw, cut the lock on the door bars, and had a man kick in the door. We changed the lock. My husband came back, kicked in the door, and cut me up with a straight razor every way but loose. I should have stayed at home with my mother and taken her beatings. I thought for sure this was her long lost son because he beat me as bad as she did.

I tried to kill myself several times. Then I got the courage to leave him and never look back. I made another vow. *No one would ever put their hands on me.* Whenever I hurt someone else, I saw only my mother and husband on the victim's face. And the damage I did was nothing nice. I was full of animosity and rage. I trusted no one. In the process, I lost a few good men because I thought beating and fighting was what made a relationship normal.

I returned to Wisconsin and started going to prison. I don't like people putting their hands on me. I've been in prison for armed robbery, reckless endangerment, forgery, party to arson, carrying concealed weapons, battery to law enforcement, disorderly conduct, resisting arrest, and absconding. All I ever wanted was someone I could love who would love me back. I met a man who used the wrong word, "love" not in my vocabulary. I started snorting black beauties and drinking all sorts of alcohol. I told my girlfriend we needed to stop drinking beer because my belly was getting bigger and swishing and moving from side to side, hurting when it did. I was twenty-three and eight months' pregnant and didn't even know it. She took me to the doctor. I found out I was having twins. I knew nothing about being a mother because I never had a mother myself.

I now have four children. I've spent most of their lives running in and out of prison and have spent a total of six years with them on the outside. I lost one daughter when she was six months old when she got caught in a heat vent. My mother tried to have me investigated for child abuse. A LOT OF NERVE. They determined it was an accident. Twenty-six days after my daughter's death, their dad died, too.

I started cashing checks, trying to bring the dead back to life. A psychic told me, "I can bring loved ones back." I believed her, and to this day, the baby I lost and their father never came back.

After that, I spent most of my life in and out of prison. I don't like anyone putting hands on my siblings or kids. My siblings still come before my kids because that's who I had to take care of and protect first.

I remarried and stayed with my man for 26 years—whenever I was out of prison, but I treated him like my first husband treated me, and he didn't deserve the sh*t I did to him. I brought my men and women home and put them in bed with us. He drank and was into drugs. I drank and smoked weed.

The outer scars have healed, but the inside ones are still quite real to me. I wear many masks because I'm afraid to discover the real me. I frighten myself when I hurt someone for putting their hands on me. My siblings talk sh*t about me for running in and out of prison, but they still come get me to fight their battles. They turned my kids against me and slept with my man. My kids are now running in and out of prison. I know nothing about being a mother because I never had an example.

The prison doctor has labeled me bi-polar, maniac depressive, post traumatic stress syndrome, and antisocial. I don't like anyone shouting at me. I miss my sister. I have grandkids I know very little about. Recently, a three-year-old granddaughter asked if I was going to spend her whole life in prison like I did her mom's. I know her mom put her up to that, and it hurts.

I still hurt inside. I put on a mask and pretend with the best of them. I search for the one thing I know I'll never find, a mother's love. I want someone to love me for me, someone to be loyal to me, someone I can trust.

I was angry at God because he let so much bad stuff happen to me. Then one day, I looked out of my prison room window, and there was this lady outside. She had a gold hue around her. She always had her Bible and acted like she was happy to be in prison. She stayed right across the hall from me. If she came my way, I'd lock myself in or sneak out of my room. One day, she cornered me and got to talking about God. I gave her all the reasons why he didn't know me and why I wasn't trying to find out anything about him. A few years later, I came across this same woman who told me to try what she had.

I got baptized April 15, 2005. I still struggle in my walk. I was having trouble forgiving. If God could forgive me, who was I to harbor anger in my heart? I learned my mother was abused and raped. I still don't like her.

If anyone says they love me, I wonder what they want from me. I don't think I'm worthy of being loved. I became obese so no one would find me appealing. I still have nightmares. Jesus wept. Who am I to think I'm too good to cry? He forgave me. Who am I to continue to harbor animosity? I sit here now living each day as if it was my last.

—⚬—

My Masks
By Star

I sit here gazing out the window
Looking at the trees so cold and bare
Realizing this is how I really feel
Cold and bare and alone.
I have felt this way much of my life.

Each branch represents
One of the many masks I wear.
I have worn them throughout the years,
Months, weeks, days, and even minutes.
If you knew me or
Sought to find the real me behind the masks,
You would find a lonely little girl
Still bearing the scars others inflicted on her
Through the years and branches of a cold cruel life,
A little girl in search of two things she has always wanted:
A mother's love and someone to love her unconditionally.

I never knew what I did to be unworthy of my own mother's love,
Or my first husband's,
To make them hate me and inflict so much pain.
All I ever wanted was someone
To please love me for me.
Was this too much to ask, to yearn for?
Apparently, because they are
Still missing from my life today.
The outer scars have healed,
But not the ones deep in my soul.
I'm cold and bare with no emotions
I can reveal, for these are all I was shown.
Animosity and bitterness are some of the daily masks I wear

To keep anyone from hurting me again.

They are very much a part of me
The cold ruthless angry woman I was forced to become.
I'm so afraid to trust others and sometimes…
I'm even afraid to trust myself—or love me.

If you could grant me a wish,
It would be for the one thing I will never find
A mother's love!
I must keep my guard up because
I'm easy prey for others to hurt, use, and abuse.
I must always question why someone is being nice to me,
Not abusing and mistreating me.
I must find their motive,
And there may be none,
But I must shield that lonely, frightened little girl
In the depths of my soul.
That's the only love I know.
No trust.
Use and abuse are the only "love"
I ever received.

I ask myself daily,
What did I do to the lady I must call mom?
I'm yearning to know why
You took a part of me away,
My little sister.
I would have stopped her from crying
As I had so many times before.
You, lady they call mom,
Took away a part of me and left
A void—emptiness, bitterness, coldness
A confused adult woman
Me.

I harbor so much anger and mistrust.
It has allowed me to have no regard for many or few.
I don't want to be this way.
And, Lord knows I want to be and have the
Love others have.
I don't like running in and out of prison,
Staring at these four walls which
Engulf my physical being.

As for my mental state,
My captors label me with their fancy terms:
Antisocial, bipolar, maniac depressive, PTSD.
Would you like to walk in my shoes?

The trees will have leaves on them.
When the seasons change
They will sprout new branches.
What about me?

Soon I'll enter back into society
And I will create another mask
To fit the labels they have placed on me.
I can't let anyone close enough to hurt me.
I'm still trying to heal the inside scars.
I'm still afraid—that same frightened young girl
I was so many years ago.
Only my pillow knows how many tears I have cried.

Can someone please help me find the real me
So I can put the masks away?
I'd put them in Pandora's Box
And never see them again.
Is it possible to save a wretch like me?

—⟋ɯ⟍—

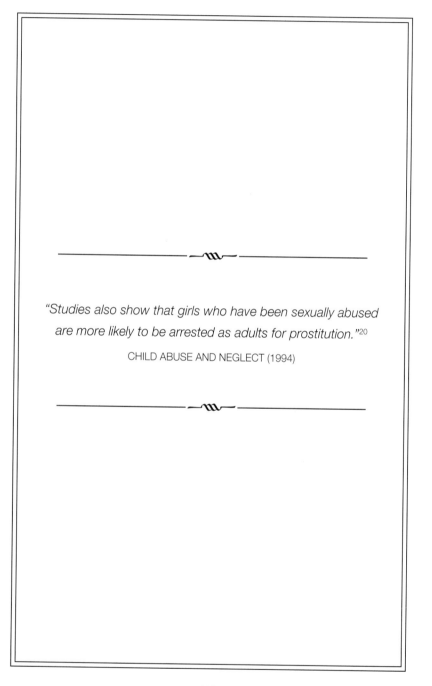

"Studies also show that girls who have been sexually abused are more likely to be arrested as adults for prostitution."[20]

CHILD ABUSE AND NEGLECT (1994)

CHAPTER 19

Lynn

———

My name is Lynn. I was raised in Milwaukee, Wisconsin, but was born in Redlake, Minnesota, on an Indian reservation. My mother went home to her family to have me after she found out my father was having an affair and the other woman was pregnant. I believe this was the beginning of my mom's dislike for me. I think every time she looked at me, I reminded her of the pain my father had caused her.

After my birth, we moved back to Milwaukee. My mother worked as a beautician to support us. She started to drink and hang out in the local taverns. She met a man who married her and ended up adopting me when I was about 2 years old. I was raised to believe he was my father. He was good to me, but there was constant fighting between my parents because they drank and spent so much time in the taverns. I always felt I was the problem and I was unwanted.

I spent most of my childhood alone, and holidays were particularly painful. My parents used a holiday as another reason to drink and hang out in bars, so we never had normal holidays like most families. It was a tradition for my mother and father to spend Christmas Eve in the tavern. They would come home drunk, and I would get to open my presents. I remember they usually refrained from fighting on that night.

I especially remember one particular Christmas Eve. I was nine years old and home alone. My mom and dad were at the tavern later than usual. My presents were under the little artificial tree and I wanted to open them, so I called the tavern and asked my mom when she was coming home. She told me to go ahead and not to call and bother them anymore. I sat there so hurt, lonely, and sad, wishing I was dead.

From that point on, I sought after things to fill the void in my life. I started experimenting with alcohol and marijuana at the age of twelve. I can't tell you how good I felt the first time I got drunk. I felt like I belonged and I didn't have a care in the world. I wanted to feel like that all the time. So I drank every chance I could.

When I was about thirteen, my mom and dad came home drunk one night and told me that my dad wasn't my real dad. They said my biological grandparents wanted to meet me. They sent me to Blue River, Wisconsin.

My grandparents lived on a small farm with chickens. They were both so loving and caring. I had never felt so wanted. My grandfather spent a lot of time with me. One night, while sleeping in the spare room, I was suddenly awakened. My grandfather was forcing himself on me. Something happened to me that night that broke my spirit. I never felt worthy or deserving of anything after that, and for some reason, I always felt it was my fault. I visited my grandparents in Blue River a few more times, but I stayed close to my grandma. I even slept with her. And I never told anyone what my grandfather did.

I started drinking more and got into a sexual relationship with a man at the age of fifteen. I was looking for something or someone to love me, accept me, or just help me feel normal. As far back as I can remember, I've always felt insecure about myself and my body. I never felt like I fit in anywhere. This man was physically abusive toward me. I ended up pregnant by him a couple of times. My parents paid for me to have abortions.

I was seventeen years old and in the bar with my mom one night. I met this man named Chuck. He asked me to dance. He paid attention to me like no other, which I believe I thought was love. He introduced me to cocaine. The first time I tried it, I fell in love with it!

At the age of nineteen, I started having children. My first was Anna, who I called my "angel." Ronald was born when I was twenty-one. I promised myself I would show love to them and spend more time with them than my parents had, and I had good intentions, but as I fell deeper into my love affair with cocaine, it became my priority. I did the same thing to my children that my parents did to me and worse.

I was in and out of my kids' lives. They were in and out of foster care. Chuck was abusive, physically and emotionally. With the guilt and shame I carried about my children, it seemed I was just living to get high.

One day, I woke up and looked in the mirror and realized that I was killing myself. I was about 100 pounds and sick of my life. I started calling around to find help. I ended up in De Paul hospital in a thirty-day treatment program. I did well and went on to a half-way house. I stayed for four months.

While in the half-way house, I met Daniel. He was a wonderful man. We got married, and he helped me get my children back. I now know that we jumped into this relationship in early recovery, at a time we were looking for something to fill the void we sought through drugs and alcohol. And when we didn't meet each other's needs, we used together.

We really did love each other, and we had times of sobriety, but something was missing. I got pregnant, and we both knew we were in no position or condition to bring a baby into our lives. We were struggling to care for Anna and Ronald who were eventually taken away because of my drug use.

When I was about eight weeks' pregnant, I came home from a three-day drug binge. Dan and I decided that I was going to have an abortion. We made an appointment for the following week. I went outside and stretched out on a lawn chair in my front yard. I felt depressed, beaten down, and hopeless. Across the street, there was a building that had been converted from a bar to a church. Some people came out and walked over to me. I don't know what made them do that. They started telling me about God and his love for me and about his son who was called Jesus. I had heard about Jesus from a neighbor when I was younger, but I thought he was just a fictional character.

As these people shared with me, I began to cry. I told them about my pregnancy, my plans for an abortion, and my drug and alcohol use. I told them my children were in foster care and I didn't want to live anymore.

They told me about God's love, and from that day, they took Dan and me under their wings. We prayed the "sinner's prayer" and accepted Christ as our Lord and Savior. Dan and I started going to the church across the street. We learned about a Christian couple who couldn't have children. I didn't have an abortion but gave birth to fraternal twin boys. I know I had those boys for that couple. You'll understand as my story goes on.

We went through a Christian adoption agency in Waukesha, Wisconsin. The woman who handled our adoption had a big effect on my faith walk. She introduced me to some wonderful people at the Assembly of God Church. Dan and I moved to Waukesha, and we got my two older children back. I got pregnant again and had a beautiful little girl named Samantha.

God has blessed me in so many ways and put people in my life to mentor and help me. I continued in and out of treatment and went to a Christian-based program called New Life for Girls. But I always ended up going back to using drugs.

The ones I loved suffered the most. My husband went to jail, my teenaged children were back in foster care, and I lost parental rights to Samantha. She now lives with her twin brothers.

The guilt and shame was overwhelming. I surrendered to the fact that I lost everything and I would never change. I felt my family and friends would be better off without me. I left Waukesha on a drug mission and moved to the south side of Milwaukee.

I started living a life of prostitution to support my habit. For a couple of years, I lived day-to-day, just to get high on crack cocaine. Nothing else mattered except smoking that pipe. I hated who I was, and often wished I was dead.

One day, I was walking the streets looking for my next trick. I had been up for many days. I was weak, tired from lack of sleep, and hungry. A car pulled up. I got in. It was my husband, Dan. He had been looking for me for some time. He took me to Waukesha where my friend Chris lived. From there I went to the hospital. If Dan had not found me, I would have hemorrhaged to death from an ectopic pregnancy.

Dan decided to take me to Muskegon, Michigan, to a program called Teen Challenge. We entered rehab together. He believed that God was going to change me. I loved Teen Challenge, and it was there I began a relationship with God. But we didn't graduate. We left after four months. I knew in my heart it was the wrong decision.

We moved to Grand Rapids, Michigan, and started our new life. Dan was a journeyman carpenter and got a really good union job working on the "S Curve" project in downtown Grand Rapids. I worked in a local restaurant. We found a wonderful church home, and they welcomed us. We lived in a condo and had two cars. In outward appearances, we had it together. I believe my husband found peace because all he ever wanted was for me to be clean, sober, and happy. Dan loved me so much. And I loved him! But I couldn't find peace within me. I was in inner turmoil all the time.

About a year into my sobriety, I relapsed one night. I hid it from Dan. It wasn't long before I was in my full-blown addiction again. My husband started using with me. I would leave him for days at a time, and I know it hurt him. When I was using, I didn't care about anyone else. All I thought about was getting money to get high.

One night, Dan and I were in a hotel getting high together. We ran out of crack so I went to make money to get some more. I was gone longer than usual. When I got back, I found my husband dead. He had hung himself in the shower.

I was in total shock and pain. It was more than I could deal with, and it gave me a reason to stay high. For the next two years, I don't think there was a day I was sober. I jumped into another relationship that I thought was love. In reality, it was drug-related, and I was afraid to be alone. We came back to Wisconsin, and our addictions followed us. The one good thing that came out of this relationship was my son Josiah.

I am forty-two years old now. My daughter Anna is twenty-two, Ronald is twenty, and Josiah is three. I am currently serving time in the Taycheedah Correctional Institution on drug-related charges.

My mother and I have reconciled. We both lost our husbands the same year. She was sober for the first time in her life, and I got to know her very well. My mother is currently in a nursing home, and she misses me. She hurt me and let me down when I was a child, but I believe that hurting people hurt other people. I've always loved her and have forgiven her. She did the best she knew how.

I miss my children, too, especially Josiah. Sometimes it hurts so much. I believe that God is molding me and making me into the mother he intended me to be in the first place. One day, He will restore my relationship with my little boy.

I know now that I have been driven by guilt. I have spent my entire life running from regrets and hiding from my shame. I believe that guilt-driven people are manipulated by memories. They allow their past to control their future. They often unconsciously punish themselves by sabotaging their own success.

God has done for me what I could not do for myself. He humbled me, pulled me out of an unhealthy relationship and the world and all of its distractions. I have tried to do things my way for too long. He had to strip me of everything and bring me to prison to get my attention. You see, you don't realize God is all you need until God is all you got.

I let the devil deceive me and confuse me. I believed the false identity placed on me from my parents and the men in my life. I knew what the Bible said, but I never believed it was for me. I was unable to receive God's love, much less his mercy and grace.

Today, I stand on God's Word and his promises, "There is no condemnation for those who are in Christ Jesus" (Romans 8:1). " I am a new creation in Christ. The old is gone, the new has come" (II Corinthians 5:17).

I've been in bondage for many years. I chose to live my life for selfish desires. God brought me to prison to set me free.

As long as I can remember, I've had a heart for women who struggle with drugs, alcohol, food, and men—probably because I could relate. I want to bring God's love to other hurting women. I have finished high school and would like to someday have a ministry for women.

I thank and praise God for not giving up on me and for saving my life. The Bible says: "For I know the plans I have for you; plans to prosper you and not to harm you, plans to give you hope and a future" (Jeremiah 29:11).

I pray that he will use me for his glory. That's what I was created for. I can hardly wait to see what he's going to do in my life!

UPDATE: I was released from prison in April 2007. My parole officer put me in a homeless shelter because there are no half-way houses for women in our city. But, I am grateful for the shelter and the help they gave me to start a new life.

My first priority was to find a job, which wasn't as easy as I thought. When you are a felon, society does not easily forgive or give you another chance. I filled out over thirty applications and didn't even get one interview. I did finally find a part-time waitress job at a restaurant where I worked prior to my last incarceration. I continued to look for full-time work.

While I was in the shelter, my mom became ill and ended up in the hospital. I wasn't expecting that. She had been on dialysis for over eight years. She was tired. I spent every day with her, not knowing if it could be the last. She passed away in June, two months after I was released. This is what I read at her funeral:

> The last time I was standing here talking was at my dad's funeral. I never had the chance to say all that I wanted to him because his death was sudden and unexpected. That wasn't the case with my mother.
>
> When I came home in April, I spent a lot of time with her, restoring our relationship. I didn't know those would be our last days...but she did. This past week, when I went to the nursing home to pick up Mom's belongings, one of the nurses shared a conversation they had. She said Mom told her she was tired and wanted to stop her kidney dialysis many months ago.
>
> The nurse asked her, "Why don't you just stop going, if that's what you want to do, Brenda?"
>
> My mom said, "No, I need to wait for my daughter to get home."
>
> And that's just what she did. Six weeks ago, Mom ended up in the hospital. She wasn't alone. I came to see her twice a day, to feed her, rub her feet, comb her hair, tell her stories and, of course, crack some jokes. I had the chance to thank her and tell her how much I loved and appreciated her. Though she wasn't one to share her feelings and emotions, she did express she was tired and ready to go. She asked me if I was gonna be okay. I assured her I would.
>
> Then she said, "Be good, Lynn."

I took that opportunity to share my faith in God and what he's done in my life. The night before she passed away, my daughter and I heard the last words she would speak.

She said, "Lord, forgive me for my sins, and Jesus save me."

Then my daughter asked her, "Will you be waiting for us in heaven, Grandma?"

Mom whispered, "Oh, yeah!"

So now I rejoice because I know for sure my mom has gone home to heaven where there is no more pain, sorrow, tears, or dialysis. Though I will miss her dearly, I have peace in my heart because I had the chance to tell her everything I wanted to. I love you, Mom.

After my mom passed away, I went through a state of depression. I had lost my husband, my dad, and my mom all within six years. In addition, my little boy, Josiah, moved to Michigan with his father. I felt so alone during this time. The St. Vincent de Paul Ministry helped me financially so I could visit my son in Michigan and that helped my depression. I also did a lot of praying and leaning on God to help me through.

I saved some money and moved out of the shelter. Looking back, it was too soon because I couldn't afford the expenses of my new apartment on a part-time job. I had added stress of supervision fees from probation and child-support. I felt overwhelmed and found myself getting into unhealthy relationships to fill the void and, I suppose, to get help financially. These choices left me feeling empty.

I continued to fill out applications for full-time work but couldn't get a break with my record. I believe I would have given up long ago if it wasn't for the financial support and encouragement of my mentors. They believed in me when I didn't believe in myself.

I moved in with my daughter and found a decent job at a dry-cleaning store in Milwaukee. I thought it was a good idea at the time but I left my support system and went back to my old stomping grounds. I went back to that unhealthy relationship I was telling you about and ended up pregnant. Within two months, I had a miscarriage and lost my uncle to cancer. I found myself depressed and drinking with family members at the funeral and landed myself back in jail for a short stay.

After my release, I went back to the homeless shelter. I found another job and another apartment. I wish I could tell you there was a happy ending, but I allowed that man back in my life. He was abusive, and when I told him it was over, he didn't handle it well. He threw rocks through my apartment window, damaged my car, and called my P.O. to make false accusations against me. She put me in jail for a week. While there, I lost another job. Then the man broke into my apartment and took my clothes, and the few things I had managed to acquire.

So now, I am back to Square One. I don't feel sorry for myself because I know it is my own fault. The choices I made in the past have influenced my life today. Maybe if I had known that, I would have done differently.

I am not giving up because I know I am a good person and a hard worker. And I have faith God is going to open a door for a decent job to support myself without any man or my vices. I just need to lean on and trust in him instead of doing it my way. But it isn't always easy.

I have a desire to start a program to help others coming out of prison. I would like to help employers see the benefits of giving us a chance. Programs like tax deductions and the Federal Bonding Program are already available. I realize we have made bad choices, but giving us a chance to work is the only way to help us stand on our own and stay away from old behaviors. I pray I can do something different. I don't want to be another statistic.

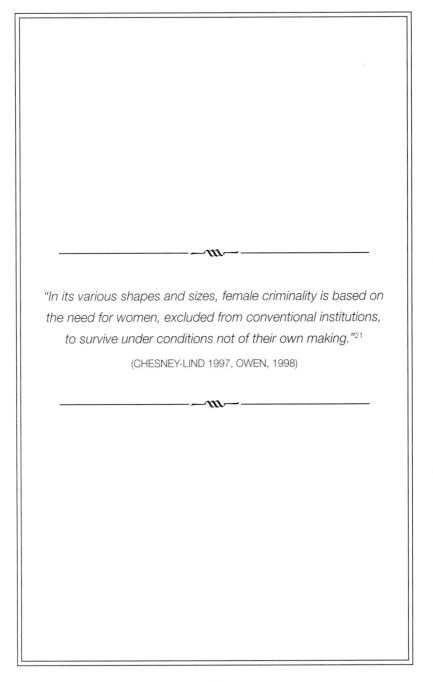

"In its various shapes and sizes, female criminality is based on the need for women, excluded from conventional institutions, to survive under conditions not of their own making."[21]

(CHESNEY-LIND 1997, OWEN, 1998)

CHAPTER 20
Yolanda

—ᴍ—

My name is Yolanda, and I was born in Chicago, Illinois, to a white mother and an Italian father. Back in those days, it was considered a mixed marriage, and couples like my parents weren't well accepted, so my mother decided to take off and leave my older sister and me with my father. Eventually, my father did the same and left us with a stranger, a woman who took us to her home in Puerto Rico. She gave my sister up for adoption. I remember her waving goodbye as she rode away in a fancy car with a strange couple. I was four years old and already knew what despair and loneliness really felt like.

I was raised by people who were total strangers. The years I lived in that house were filled with physical, emotional, mental, and sexual abuse. The physical abuse started with my so-called mother. The sexual molestation began at the age of six from my so-called father. But then my older, so-called brothers began their sexual abuse and rape. There were eight of them. I lived in constant fear because I never knew who was going to spend the night in my bed.

I used to hide in the outhouse all night or in the roof of the house, but the physical abuse after they found me and dragged me back in was unbearable. They intimidated me and forced me to do what they wanted by beating me down with leather belts, water hoses, wire, or cable. The one that scared me the most was a big machete. I have scars on my body from those horrible memories.

By the age of nine I knew everything I needed to know about sex, alcohol, and drugs because it was easier for me to be intoxicated than deal with my life the way it was. I became a very young "woman" because, just like a wife, I was in charge of the cleaning and cooking, and when the night came, I was someone's sexual partner. I hated my life.

Finally, when I was eleven, my so-called father passed away from a lung disease. I was very happy because one of them was out of my life. I could never understand why my so-called mother never defended me from those monsters. There were many times I screamed from the top of my lungs for help and she closed the bedroom door, pretending not to hear. Even a neighbor heard me and came a few times to my defense.

A few years later, my so-called mother passed away from a heart attack. She died right in my arms, confessing to me that she wasn't my real mother after all. I finally understood why she never loved me.

A week later, one of my so-called brothers threw me out of the house because I fought them hard every time they came after me. I was too big and grown to let them control me like they had. I decided I was no longer their slave. So, I was on the street alone.

No more abuse, I thought. *From now on, I will defend myself, and I will never let anyone else hurt me again.*

But life on the streets has its own agenda, and I was too young and too naïve. I was only thirteen-years old and I did just about everything to survive. And this is where I saw the work of God, protecting me every step of the way. Life on the street is cruel, hard, and without mercy.

One day, God put a pastor and his family in my life. I was working in a pineapple field, and they came to purchase some pineapples for an activity at their church. I had the honor to serve them that day, and from then on they offered me a place to stay and work. They owned a hardware store, and I became their dog-keeper. I was scared at first. Those were some big dogs, and they looked like beasts instead of dogs, but I needed the job, and more important, a place to stay. I was tired of running the streets and horrified about the way life was. I earned my way into this family's home and their dogs' hearts. I got so close to their dogs that I spent my nights sleeping in the doghouse with them. This was the first lesson of love that I ever had.

Late one evening, the oldest of my so-called brothers came looking for me to take me back home. He tried to get a hold of me, and one of the dogs jumped on him and knocked him out. The other one took a bite of his stomach. It was gross, but they defended me, and that was all that mattered. The dogs became my best friends

So, that was my life. I went to school during the day and lived with my dogs at night until my pastor decided to set me up to marry a good candidate from the church. I was sixteen-years old. I felt I owed them, so I followed their lead. Inside I was scared to death. Two months later, I was married at the church. We had a huge reception but the most sour honeymoon anyone could imagine. My husband found out I was not a virgin, and in the Spanish community that is a very big deal. He did not know anything about my past, and of course, when I did try to explain to him the kind of life I lived, it was too late.

My past was unacceptable to him. He was too involved in the community. He wanted to keep everything a secret, so we continued living our life as a happy family in front of everyone. In the privacy of our home it was hell. His demands for sexual satisfaction were repugnant, and the physical abuse and violence began the minute I said "no" to his demands.

After four years of hardship and despair, there was one final beating that almost killed me. While I was in a hospital, the police arrested my ex-husband and kept him in jail long enough for me to escape the country with my kids.

I came back to the United States looking for a new beginning with three little kids and no English. But the grace of God is bigger than anyone can imagine. My success had no limits in school, work, and home. Life was good, and I forgot that God had helped me every step of the way. I became arrogant and self-centered.

In 2001 my youngest daughter was brutally raped at the age of sixteen. From there, my life began to go downhill again. With such a tragedy, the family was torn apart. My daughter became depressed, and nothing seemed to help. I felt guilty and helpless. We tried to work things out. Two years later, we found out she was HIV positive from the rape.

Our lives took a turn for the worse. I refused to accept that such a tragedy was happening to my dear daughter, and I was very angry at God for not protecting her. I began to blame him for all my misfortune instead of having faith. I wanted to save her. I found myself selling everything I owned and stealing to pay for medical treatment after medical treatment. Nothing made a difference.

My daughter turned to drugs as a coping method, and I pretty much did the same because I drank my sorrow away. When I could drink no more, I used cocaine to bring myself up so I could continue drinking day after day. And I watched my daughter destroying herself because we both gave up.

She committed suicide on January 7, 2008, after finding out that I was facing prison time for the crimes I had committed. There was one final chance that I had to save her life, a very expensive transplant treatment. In my desperation I refused to see that my daughter did not want to go on.

I scheduled the treatment anyway. On the day of the surgery, early in the morning, she waited until all her blood testing was done. Then she went into the bathroom and shot up some heroin. The doctor took her up for her surgery. Minutes later, he returned to give me the news that my daughter had passed away due to an overdose. The combination of the anesthesia and the heroin produced a heart attack that killed her instantly.

I was confused and devastated. Hours later, I went home, and while I was laying on my bed crying and screaming into my pillow because I didn't want anyone to hear me, I found a letter that my daughter left for me.

Dear Mom:

Please find it in your heart to forgive me for what I have done, for all the troubles I have caused and the financial burden I have put you through that forced you to commit those crimes. But all of that wasn't necessary. You see, Mom, I was dead the day I was raped by that animal. He took my life with him then, and there was nothing you could have said or done. I will always love you, and maybe, if God is who he is, I know that I will see you one day, because he promised me that. But you have to promise me to be good and to let God help you so I can see you again. I am sorry again, Mom, but I am in peace now, and you need to do what you have to do so you can also find peace. Thank you for loving me the way you did, and please know that I did love you, too.

See ya!
Mariposa (my daughter's nickname in Spanish which translates to butterfly)

Shortly after her death, I was sentenced to eighteen months of straight time in jail. I began serving my sentence on July 3, 2008, and spent a lot of time in cell restriction because I wanted to die. I felt empty, and I couldn't find anything to live for. I hated my life. I hated me, and what I had become—a cold monster with no feelings. I cared for nothing and nobody.

I was not allowed to attend Mariposa's funeral because it was out of the country. My ex-husband paid for it. It was ironic because he was never involved in my children's lives; in fact he denied my daughter because she didn't look like him. She was blonde and had blue eyes like my biological mother. He was willing to pay for the funeral as a direct punishment to me, knowing that I would not be allowed to leave the country with open criminal cases.

My other children were so mad at me, they weren't speaking to me because of my crimes. I felt I had lost all of them instead of one and that included my grandchildren. I didn't have anyone else, or so I thought. During all the time spent in cell restriction, fighting with the correctional officers and inmates, God found the way to speak to me because he has a purpose and a plan for our lives.

There was this lady at the jail facility that took the time to bring me a message, the Message of all messages.

She told me there is hope for the people who seek God and ask for forgiveness because Jesus, the Son of God, has cleaned and wiped our sins away at the cross. All I had to do was accept that he died for my sins and I would receive the gift of eternal life. She also said my life had been a huge test that would turn into a great testimony because that is what God wanted me to do.

From that point on, I decided my life wasn't worth living without God. I also decided that I had always lived my life the way I wanted to live it and it never worked out—not for me, not for my love ones. It was time to let God handle my life. It couldn't be any worse than what I had lived so far.

Here I am, sixteen months later, and I could scream out loud that I have never been this free in my life. Even though I am still incarcerated, now in a Huber facility with working privileges, God is blessing my life in so many ways. I have my family back. I am working and going to school to become a counselor for alcohol and domestic abuse victims and youth welfare, because I want to be able to pass on the message that I got when I needed it the most.

I was able to confess that I had a prison within me and handed all my problems and sorrows to God. And He took every single one of them so I don't feel alone anymore. He is with me. He gave me my family back, and we have learned a new way to love each other. It is a great feeling.

God is not promising a life without storms, but he does promise to help us through it. He filled my heart with hope, love, and faith. There is no space for sorrow and loneliness. He has opened doors for my future, and every day I get friendly reminders that God is in my life. He is there whether we look for him or not, because he loves us no matter what. His unconditional love is always there when we need it. He constantly reminds me that if I face a big mountain of troubles, he is bigger than that mountain!

I hope my story will serve as an inspiration for all of you ladies out there that struggle with hardship and despair. There is only one way out of it, the way of hope that takes us to the path of new life in Jesus our Savior and everlasting life with God.

Thank you for reading my story. I am praying that every person who reads it will be touched and strengthened by the Holy Spirit. I also pray you will find blessings in your life and you will believe that with God everything is possible. God bless!!!

Yolanda Lee

—m—

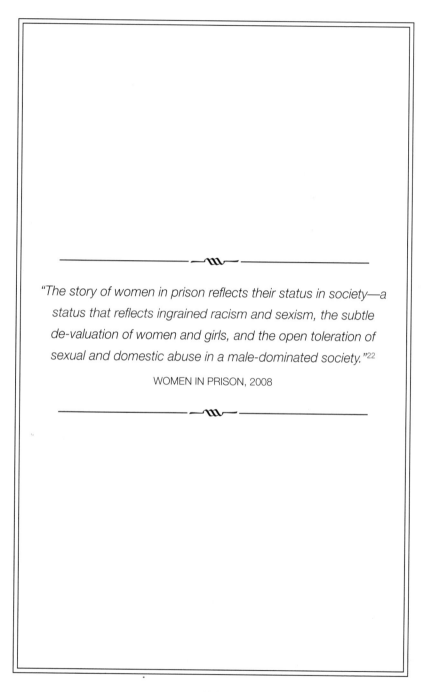

"The story of women in prison reflects their status in society—a status that reflects ingrained racism and sexism, the subtle de-valuation of women and girls, and the open toleration of sexual and domestic abuse in a male-dominated society."[22]

WOMEN IN PRISON, 2008

CHAPTER 21

Ann

—⁓⁓—

*M*y experience changed my life. I will not ever be the person I was before jail, not that it is a bad thing. I guess it just is what it is now. I am a divorced mother of three beautiful children. My story starts in 2005 and is not unlike the story of many victims of abuse who are re-victimized by the very system that was designed to protect them. This situation is not an isolated event. My teenage daughter was sexually assaulted on Halloween 2005. She was an honor student, not a child of the streets. A member of a well-known gang raped her.

Immediately, we were referred to the Women's Center to begin the process of healing. While in counseling, my daughter started having flashbacks and nightmares. She couldn't sleep and could not really function. I learned that sometimes trauma brings forth more trauma. She finally disclosed that her estranged father had abused her.

You try to make sense out of some things that don't make sense. You never believe this could happen to your child. We were in turmoil. We were in shock. Honestly, I do not think there is anything more devastating than watching as your own children are consumed by this type of pain.

My daughter's statement about her father was video taped by Human Services and the prosecution of the gang member proceeded. I suggested to my daughter that it would be good for her to attend the sentencing hearing of the gang member because I thought it would give her a chance to stand before him and say what she wanted to say.

In the meantime her estranged father, who was under investigation for abusing her, wrote a letter to the rapist's defense attorney. Her father's letter, which was read aloud in court stated, "She had it coming."

I wondered, "Why did the district attorney allow such a letter to be read? And what kind of a person writes a letter in defense of his own child's rapist?" I was shocked, and my daughter was absolutely devastated. It shows you birds of a feather do really flock together!

We tried to move on from this horror. My estranged husband started a campaign to ruin the reputation of both my daughter and me. He wanted the investigating detective, a woman, to believe we made it up. Sexual abusers often blame their victims, and most abusers instill incredible fear so their victims end up believing it is "their fault."

He went to the woman detective assigned to be investigating him and filed six different police reports against my daughter [the victim] and myself, stating we threatened to make up stories and say that he molested her. I never thought that this detective would end up being completely manipulated, but she was.

He also filed reports stating we were "harassing him via phone." It was really unbelievable. The detective never even bothered to investigate! Had she taken the time to actually check the phone records, she would have learned that he was lying and we were not calling him. We had been divorced for 10 years, and there was very little contact since 2002 due to domestic violence.

The final report filed by my ex-husband resulted in criminal charges against me with my daughter listed as "a juvenile suspect." We were accused of filling out an application on the Internet for a credit card using his last name and my first name. Then he claimed the denied application was sent to his address. The entire case was based on him walking "a letter" from a credit agency into that detective's office and telling her he had received it, and it represented evidence of what "we" had done. It was so crazy. Why would I send an illegal credit application to his address?

I still believed in the system back then, so I thought it was not a big deal. I figured the court would see through the whole thing and realize this was his attempt to take the focus off his prosecution for what he did to his daughter.

Well, that type of thinking was really naïve, because the system is broken. My experience taught me that sometimes prosecution becomes all about "winning at all costs." It really has very little to do with justice. It was very disappointing and shameful.

I got lost in trying to prove my innocence. How could this happen? I didn't even have the Internet at home. For the next two years I learned computers inside and out, trying to trace the data that would prove I did not apply for that credit card. I thought that somehow after I proved we did not do this, the police would seek justice on behalf of my daughter. I was wrong.

None of it mattered to anyone within the system. I had become a pain and nuisance to those involved who were supposed to protect my daughter. In the process, I tried to cope and numb the pain with prescription pills. I got to the point where I was awake four to five days in a row, not eating or sleeping, and this had consumed my life. I pretty much wanted to die.

In March 2008 I showed up for trial and was told that it would be in my best interest to plea to disorderly conduct so I could just pay a fine and move on. If we went to trial and people did not understand the Internet, we might lose. Then I would be sentenced to prison.

It really bothered me. First, I did not do this, and second, there had not even been a crime committed. In all actuality the statute I was charged under clearly stated, "something of value must be obtained" before one is supposed to be charged. In addition, the supposed letter that my ex-husband gave to the detective was not even legitimate, which explains why I could not find any data on the Internet. And the credit card company said they faxed this information to the district attorney's office. The letter was faxed to the district attorneys office because its credibility was questionable. It did not contain the registered trademark of the credit card company, and the logo was wrong. It looked as if it had been cut and pasted from a computer. But I guess at that point it didn't matter. I believe I was prosecuted because either they just did not like me, or it was truly about "winning at all costs."

No one thought about what this was doing to my children or to me. The harder I pushed, stressed out beyond belief, the weirder it all got. My attorney said things like, "The prosecutor says that you are a stalker. The prosecutor said that you have just never moved on after your divorce and maybe you are jealous of your ex-husband."

I felt so defeated and really misunderstood. If only somebody would have slowed down enough to realize that they were making fun of me at the expense of my children's pain. If only they would have looked at the one person who abused my daughter without consequences. Needless to say, my daughter's abuser succeeded in shifting the focus from his crime to accusations against us, and he was never held accountable.

I had agreed to pay a fine to disorderly conduct and move on. I realized I had not been doing anything good for my kids or myself by trying to convince someone to help us and in fact was just wasting years caught up in the system, trying to prove something that in the end did not matter.

I think that is what bothers me most. It is all the wasted time that really hurt us, and I cannot ever get back that time taken from my children. It was not fair. Instead of paying a fine, the judge sent me to jail for six months and told me not to make any more false claims against my ex husband, "the victim." It still keeps me up at night. I wonder why the judge said that?

It bothers me because all the progress and the courage it took for my daughter to come forward regarding what happened to her was literally taken back and stomped on by the very system meant to protect her. While I was hauled off to jail, everyone, including the system, just assumed that someone would step up and take responsibility for my three children and their lives. Wrong. My children were left alone to fend for themselves while I sat in jail, helpless and hopeless. I told my attorney who did nothing. I told the guards who did nothing.

In fact one guard told me, "I do not like you or your personality and, hey, you are not in a position to do anything for your kids now, are you?"

My daughter felt like this was her fault because she came forward. My younger children just felt scared because I am all they have ever had. None of this was their fault. They have been violated. They paid the price. Their lives were altered. They do not trust the world around them. They do not feel safe. They will not ever turn to the police for help. It is not okay.

My daughter did take care of her younger brother and sister while I was incarcerated. She paid the bills, did the housework, worked part time, ran errands, grocery shopped, and dealt with everything, all while finishing high school. She was forced to give up any possibility of being a regular kid during the last year of high school.

She is my hero. She completed four years of high school in three and graduated with honors. She is now in college majoring in chemistry and will eventually receive her doctorate in pharmacy. Most of all, she is at peace and she is happy.

It is hard to believe in this 21st century: crimes of sexual violence are still being hushed up. And when a victim comes forward, the system allows more abuse in the form of retaliation. The response by those in authority is often inappropriate and hostile. When you think about it, that's the best insurance policy an abuser can have, protection against detection and prosecution. That man, who had the audacity to hurt this beautiful person and drag us through all of this, cannot hurt her anymore. Forgiving him set us free.

It has been one full year since being released from jail, and it is really hard trying to rebuild both financially and emotionally. We were literally without any money. I had a very hard time finding a job. People do discriminate against people with a criminal record, and it was very difficult to hold on and try to find the strength to convince someone that I was worthy of a chance to be able to do more than just exist. Emotionally, it is really hard to overcome the shame and humiliation instilled while in jail. I felt completely degraded and gross. However, I have been determined to push forward and succeed because I want my kids to have faith and hope.

For the most part, finding a job has been the key to truly being able to feel a little better. And it is not just about having money to cover the bills because we have lived without any money and we were happy with each other. There are worse things that can happen in life than running out of money. It is about getting up every day and having a routine, about being able to go to work, and contribute to the community.

This experience taught me the most difficult lessons in life are based in spirituality. I have learned how to return love for hate, how to include the excluded, how to forgive without apology, and how to say I was wrong. It is next to impossible to explain this to anyone, and people look at me like I am crazy when I say this experience has made me a better person.

Some good came from this nightmare. Even though we were completely broken and without hope, God never failed us, and I know he watched over my kids when there was no one else that cared. He has never let go. While in jail, I stopped taking the prescription pills and have literally felt renewed. I love life and do not take any days for granted. My faith is strong, and it is the good that came from the bad.

Rising above it, moving forward, learning to forgive. That is justice.

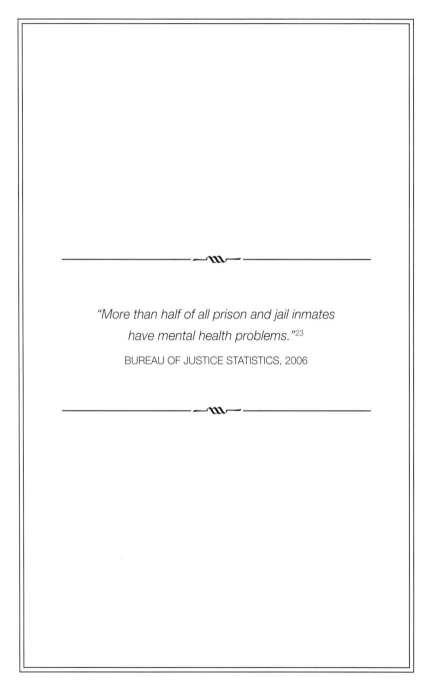

"*More than half of all prison and jail inmates have mental health problems.*"[23]

BUREAU OF JUSTICE STATISTICS, 2006

CHAPTER 22

Tesa

—⚒—

I was born in Milwaukee, Wisconsin, in 1969. My parents were both college-educated. Dad was in the army, and when I was three weeks old, we relocated to another state.

There were three of us kids, my two older brothers and myself. We are all three years apart with three different dads. (Lots of threes huh?) When I was three years old, my parents moved back to the Midwest and became police officers in a large metropolitan community.

We went to church and lived in a nice neighborhood where people owned their own homes and took pride in their properties. My parents provided well for my material needs, so I lacked nothing. Emotionally, I lacked everything.

There were times when my parents were working and left me in the care of a colleague of theirs, another officer who had a daughter. I was forced to call him "uncle." Beginning at the age of four until I was eight years old, the bastard repeatedly beat and raped me. I remember thinking, "Who do you tell when the people who are supposed to protect you are hurting you?"

I began spending a lot of time with my grandparents. My mom became addicted to opiates and was forced to resign from her job on the police force. I saw my parents less and less. Eventually, they divorced.

My grandparents worked full-time so I became the responsible one, cooking and cleaning for my brothers, even helping them with their home-work. Though I was the youngest, I was always a bit advanced for my age.

My grandfather believed in education, but back then, it was not so important to me. In hindsight, I wish I could have listened more intently. School was good until I discovered drugs—and then I discovered there was a profit to be made.

I became addicted to cocaine at the age of ten, went to my first treatment facility at eleven, and my first psychiatric hospitalization by twelve. I dropped out of high school at the age of fifteen due to an unplanned pregnancy. Eventually, I completed my General Education Diploma at an area technical college. My history with drugs continued until I was labeled with PTSD, childhood trauma, and manic depression.

My drug abuse continued through the years. I was a functioning addict and was able to raise my daughter and see her graduate from high school. She received an award at graduation—something about "beating the odds." I was very involved in her education because I knew it would be one of the only things that could break the cycle of our family dysfunction. Raising a child, I now understood what my grandparents and parents wanted for me.

After my daughter graduated, I was arrested and convicted for selling narcotics. I went to prison for twenty-two months at Taycheedah, Wisconsin's maximum security women's prison. There I learned, and started to believe, that I did not have to leave a legacy of despair and pain for my future generations. That is where I made a full-hearted decision to turn my will and my life over to the care of God, as I understood him.

I went back to school while I was in prison and earned an Office Software Application Certificate. In addition, I made plans to further my education when I got out. Well, all that sounds good and dandy. However, I had to do some more experimenting with drugs, and that lasted about six of the twelve months I had on parole.

Strangest thing, though, I got off of parole April 19, 2008, but did not make a life-altering decision until May 22, 2008, when I decided to do something about the trauma that always brought me back to using. See, I thought I deserved to "get high" because of all of the pain I lived through. I honestly thought I deserved to destroy my life and others because I was a victim.

Well, screw that. I may have had things happen to me, but that does not mean I had to be stagnant for the rest of my years. I got counseling at the Women's Center and AODA counseling, as well. They educated me on the subjects that were causing distress in my life. Through this experience, I came to understand how to deal with things like night terrors, triggers, and depression. While I still suffer on occasion, I have one heck of a support system and a plan.

Despite their faults, my grandparents and parents instilled core values, ethics, and morals in me, which I feed off of today. In the here and now, I realize I had to make some mistakes to become who I am. My favorite saying is, "Respect the past, don't live in it."

In conclusion, I have decided that education is one of the key components in combating recidivism into jails and institutions. Now I make school my Number One priority.

Being in class has boosted my self-esteem and heightened my feeling of self-worth. I plan to continue until I receive my doctorate. I have my sights set on Harvard. I may be in a wheelchair by the time I make it, and I won't be disappointed if I never do because I know that I have given it my best.

—◈—

---⟋m⟍--- ---

"The historic role of the church combined with its potential for volunteer resources uniquely position the faith community to support the successful reintegration of returning prisoners."[24]

DEPARTMENT OF HEALTH AND HUMAN SERVICES, USA

---⟋m⟍--- ---

A Brief Guide to Jail & Prison Ministry

—⟋⟍⟍—

WHY JAIL AND PRISON MINISTRY?

*T*he United States leads the world in producing prisoners. According to the Bureau of Justice Statistics, in 2008 there were 7.3 million people under the supervision of the correctional system (locked up, on probation or on parole). That's one out of every thirty-one adults. Eighty-five percent of these individuals are non-violent offenders who will eventually return home to live in our communities.

Whether we pay higher prices for goods and services as a result of theft or come into direct contact with someone who has committed a crime, all of us are affected in some way by the actions and decisions of these individuals. We can no longer live with the illusion that if we just put enough bad people behind bars, our society will be safe. The current trend is to build more prisons and fill them until they are overflowing. Then, to alleviate the crowded conditions and high costs of caring for non-violent offenders, we send them back to the community with the same problems and coping skills that got them in trouble in the first place.

The barriers to successful re-integration are overwhelming for offenders who lack basic education and job skills. Even minimum wage jobs can be out of reach for individuals with a criminal record. An offender can lose everything while incarcerated. Unless there is a family and a job waiting for her, it is unlikely she will secure shelter, furniture, transportation, and medical care without the help of community agencies.

One inmate told me, "I'm going to be released next week. It should be the happiest day of my life, and all I can think about is, 'Sh* t, where am I going to sleep?'"

I have seen inmates go through this process multiple times. If a woman has exhausted all of her options for free resources, she may choose to return to an abusive partner who pays the rent and most likely got her in trouble in the first place. If that is not an option, the more resourceful woman will survive the only way she knows how: stealing, selling drugs, or selling herself. If arrested again, she becomes another statistic in a process called recidivism.

CAN ONE PERSON REALLY MAKE A DIFFERENCE?

*T*he answer is "yes." Like Father Joe, I have seen people turn their lives around because someone cared enough to mentor them. We will not heal every hurt or find a solution to every problem. But I believe Jesus calls us to love the unlovable, share the Gospel, and show mercy to everyone touched by the criminal justice system. The outcome is not our responsibility. The healing comes from him.

Some offenders will seem to suck the life out of you because their needs are so great. You will not be able to meet all of those needs. Love them, pray for them, and don't expect to fix their circumstances. Work with an established ministry for direction and discernment.

It is important to take care of yourself. Ministry can be an exhausting and, at the same time, an uplifting experience. You need to surround yourself with others who will hold you in prayer. God will give you the strength you need if you spend time with him and renew yourself.

WHAT CAN I DO TO HELP?

*W*hen I asked the women how people can help them, they always answered, "Pray for us and our families."

If God has given you a heart for this ministry, start with prayer. And if prayer is the only thing you ever do, you have made an important contribution. Remember, this is spiritual warfare, and those who fight the battle need guidance and strength. If your gift is prayer, consider the following needs:

- Pray for prisoners and their families.
- Pray for the safety of correctional officers who care for the imprisoned.
- Pray that inmates will be granted access to religious freedom.
- Pray that prison officials will allow faith-based programming for life skills, drug treatment, parenting skills, anger management, and re-entry planning.
- Ask God to transform lives through these programs.
- Pray that Bibles and other religious materials will be available to inmates.
- Pray for those in ministry.
- Pray for victims of crime and their families.
- Pray for a spirit of healing and forgiveness to those affected by crime.

- Pray that mentors will stay in contact with prisoners after their release.
- Pray for reform in the criminal justice system.
- Pray for equal access to medical and mental-health treatment for offenders.
- Ask God for guidance in how to use the gifts he has given you.

CAN I JUST MAKE A DONATION?

*M*any organizations that support jail and prison ministry accept donations. If there is a correctional facility in your community, contact the prison chaplain for specific needs. Each institution has its own set of rules. Some are in need of hygiene kits, books for the library (ask what is acceptable), Bibles, and devotional materials.

There is always a need for financial support but it is never a good idea to give money directly to an individual inmate. Our ministry (St. Vincent de Paul) is supported by donations and provides eye exams, eyeglasses, Bibles, new games and puzzles, haircuts, movies, DVD players, books, holiday treats, and other items requested by the jail. Our aftercare programs offer bus passes, food, clothing, household items, and rent assistance.

There are many non-profit organizations and churches that help prisoners and their families, but be cautious and check them out thoroughly before giving your money. Some are listed in Appendix A. To find groups in your area, search on line for "prison ministries."

WHAT ABOUT WRITING TO A PRISONER?

*Y*ou can make a difference, even save a life, without ever leaving home. Men and women serving time are very lonely. Some individuals get no mail and no visitors. They may be separated from family and friends due to geographic location or a break in family ties. Please understand I am not promoting dating relationships, which, unfortunately, are the focus of some pen pal services. A Christian friendship can do much to encourage a positive attitude and a desire for change.

Your church might want to form its own pen pal ministry. This is an opportunity to mentor neighbors and members of the congregation who are in need of support and prayer. It's a good idea to use the church address or a personal P.O. box for return mail. You can even use another name if you do not know the person you are mentoring.

Always use caution in communicating with prisoners. It is important to learn from people who are familiar with the prison system and the behaviors of criminals. Choose wisely. Seek out an organization that is well established and has a healthy focus.

Newsletters are another way to mentor prisoners. One couple in our ministry writes a monthly paper called Soul Food, and a volunteer pays for the postage to mail it. The project began ten years ago when a prisoner wrote to Joan asking if her church had a spiritual newsletter.

Joan told me, "When Dwain and I read the letter, we looked at each other and said, 'We can do this!'"

Soul Food now blesses over 200 inmates. Each issue of the newsletter has a central theme, such as 'prayer' or 'forgiveness,' and includes Bible studies, verses to memorize, word puzzles, and quotes from spiritual resources.

WHICH MINISTRY IS RIGHT FOR ME?

*T*here are many excellent programs to choose from. Not all of them are religious organizations, but most community agencies, such as food pantries and shelters, serve prisoners and their families on a regular basis. Start with a personal inventory. Decide what talents you would like to use. Then contact several local ministries or community agencies and explore their needs. God will place a call on your heart and match your gift to the need.

Here are some areas to consider:

- Teaching – Volunteer to help with high-school equivalency classes at your local jail or technical college. Teach someone to read through literacy programs. Tutor children at risk. Many of them have a parent in prison.
- Cooking and meal preparation – Local food pantries, meal sites, and shelters all have a need for food and volunteers. Ex-offenders are among those served.
- Car repair – Transportation is expensive and not every job can be accessed from a bus line. Many individuals need a reliable car in order to take care of their families and keep a job. Gas cards are always a welcome donation.
- Job coaching – Ex-offenders can use your help finding companies

who will hire them, writing resumes, filling out applications, and coaching for interviews.

- Religious programs – Lead a Bible study or help with Sunday services inside the jail or prison.
- Adopt a prisoner – Ask your church if they would consider adopting an ex-offender to help them become self-supporting. They will need assistance with employment, food, housing, transportation and possibly childcare.
- The arts – Bless others with your artistic talents. Provide music for worship, lead a drum circle, teach an art class, or put on a play.
- Counseling – Qualified individuals are needed for AODA counseling, anger management, parenting skills, budgeting, and after-care support groups.
- Medical services – Volunteer at a free clinic.
- Mental health – Mentally ill individuals are being incarcerated at increasingly greater numbers because of lack of services in the community. These men and women often have undiagnosed and untreated mental-health issues. They need help to access mental-health services and apply for Social Security disability and insurance programs.
- Restorative justice – Volunteers are needed for this Biblical approach to justice which brings victims, offenders, and the community together to repair the harm caused by crime.
- Public policy – Get involved in changing the system. Support equal housing programs, lobby for the rights of persons with mental illness, encourage community leaders to initiate programs such as treatment instead of prison and alcohol courts.

If you look at the big picture, you might say, "What's the use? How can one person possibly make a difference?" I don't believe God expects any of us to solve all the problems of the imprisoned. He just wants us to show them his mercy, and we can each do that, one person at a time. One letter, one prayer, one visit, one bag of groceries, that's how Jesus loves all people through us.

Like the song says, "God can use us anywhere!"

Ministry Prayer

Dear God,
You who make the sun to shine and the rain to fall upon saints and sinners alike, accept us sinners as instruments in your care of the imprisoned.

Dwell in us. Fill us with your love. Help us to see the inmates as our brothers and sisters, ours not to judge or punish, but simply to love. Let your forgiveness and healing flow through us.

Hold the inmates in your gentle hands in their time of trial. Guide them to a new life through prayer and reading of your Holy Word. Help them to remember their dignity as your children.

Lord, please give the grace of forgiveness and strength to the families of inmates. Console innocent victims of their crimes. Take all thoughts of bitterness and vengeance from their hearts.

Please bless the women and men of the jail staff. Inspire them with wisdom and patience in their difficult ministry. Keep them safe. Give them satisfaction as they model your fatherhood in gentleness and justice to the inmates.

Help us to honor the presence of your Son, Jesus, in the churches of all Christian traditions with whom we serve. Help us to cherish and respect your children of other religions. In your time, give them the Holy Spirit to know Jesus who has saved them.

Bless the leaders of our churches. Bless our fellow Vincentians working in other parts of your vineyard.

Thanks again, Lord, for the privilege to serve your children, the body of your son, Jesus, in jail.

We pray this in His holy name. *Amen.*

JOSEPH WANNER (PAPA JOE)
1930 - 2008

Appendix A – Prison and Jail Ministry Organizations

Bible Believers Fellowship, Inc.
A non-denominational Christian prison ministry that provides literature to prison chaplains and counseling and encouragement to inmates.

P.O. Box 0065
Baldwin, NY 11510-0065
Phone: 516.739.7746
www.prisonministry.org

Christian Association For Prison Aftercare
A national resource for non-profit organizations and churches that serve prisoners.

40 Hague Street, Suite 201
Detroit, MI 48202-2119
Phone: 313.875.3883
www.capaassociation.org

Good News Jail and Prison Ministry
Provides missionary chaplains, visitation, Bible correspondence courses, and small group studies to jails and prisons on five continents.

2230 E. Parham Road
Henrico, VA 23228-2226
Toll Free Phone: 1.800.220.2202
www.goodnewsjail.org

Kairos Prison Ministry International, Inc.
Volunteers from many Christian denominations minister to incarcerated individuals, their families, and those who work with them.

6903 University Blvd.,
Winter Park, FL 32792
Phone: 407.629.4948
Fax: 407.629.2668
www.kairosprisonministry.org

Letters For The Lord Prison Ministry
This is a letter ministry to inmates and their family members around the country, offering new life in Jesus Christ and Christian friendship and support.

PO Box 593
Harrah, OK 73045-0593
www.prisonministry.net/Letters

Prison Fellowship
Founder Chuck Colson. A nation-wide organization that partners with local churches and ministers to inmates and their families both during and after incarceration.

44180 Riverside Parkway
Lansdowne, VA 20176
www.prisonfellowship.org

Project Angel Tree
A division of Prison Fellowship
Angel Tree is a ministry that reaches out to inmates and their families with the love of Christ. It provides Christmas gifts to children of inmates and seeks to transform the lives of these families and to reconcile them to their Heavenly Father and each other.

National Association for the Mentally Ill (NAMI)
Grassroots mental health advocacy organization dedicated to improving the lives of individuals and families affected by mental illness.

3803 N. Fairfax Drive, Ste. 100
Arlington, VA 22203
Phone: 703.524.7600
www.nami.org

Restorative Justice Ministries Network of North America
An interdenominational criminal justice ministry. Restorative justice is a process for all the parties affected by a crime to collectively seek ways to recover from the resulting trauma.

1229 Avenue J, Suite 360
Huntsville, TX 77340
Phone: 936.291.2156
www.rjmn.net

Restorative Justice Online
Prison Fellowship International
www.restorativejustice.org

Teen Challenge International, USA
Applies Biblical principles to provide youth, adults and families with an effective and comprehensive Christian faith-based solution to life-controlling drug and alcohol problems.

5250 N. Towne Center Dr.
Ozark, MO 65721
Phone: 417.581.2181
www.teenchallengeusa.com

The National Resource Center on Children & Families of the Incarcerated (NRCCFI) at Family and Corrections Network (FCN)

93 Old York Road, Suite 1, #510
Jenkintown, PA 19046
Phone: 215.-576.1110
www.fcnetwork.org

WriteAPrisoner.com

This organization approaches the problem of recidivism through positive relationships between inmates and free citizens. It also provides current information on prison-related issues. Check out their suggestions for letter writing content.

P.O. Box 10
Edgewater, FL 32132
www.writeaprisoner.com

—⟋⟍—

References:

Chapter 1: The Block
[1] "More than 200,000 women are in prison and jail in the United States, and one million women are under criminal justice supervision."

Quick Facts: Women & Criminal Justice – 2009, Institute on Women and Criminal Justice, Women's Prison Association, www.wpaonline.org.

Chapter 2: Papa Joe
[2] "The United States has less than 5 percent of the world's population but leads the world in producing prisoners –2.3 million or one-fourth of the world's prison population."

International Center for Prison Studies, King's College, London.

Chapter 3: Standing In The Gap
[3] "Women are the fastest growing and least violent segment of prison and jail populations. 85% of female jail inmates are behind bars for non-violent offenses."

Washington DC: Justice Policy Institute, March 1999.

Chapter 4: The Search
[4] "The number of women incarcerated in prisons and jails in the United States is approximately ten times more than the number of women incarcerated in Western European countries even though Western Europe's combined female population is about the same size as that of the U.S."

Amnesty International, *Not Part of My Sentence: Violations of the Human Rights of Women in Custody*, Washington DC: Amnesty International, March 1999, p.15.

Chapter 5: In A Family Way
[5] "In 2007 more than 1.7 million children had a parent in prison or jail."

Mauer, M., A.Nellis, S. Schirmir, *Incarcerated Parents and Their Children – Trends 1991 – 2007*, The Sentencing Project, Feb. 2009 –

Chapter 6: Our Girls
[6] "Women tend to commit less violent offenses, and are more known for committing what are commonly referred to as female offenses: prostitution, embezzlement, forgery, and counterfeiting.

Institute for Public Safety and Justice Fact Sheet, 2001.

Chapter 7: The Clothesline Project
[7] "In New York, a 1999 study of female inmates at Bedford Hills Correctional Facility found that over 80% of women prisoners had a childhood history of physical

and sexual abuse, and more than 90% had experienced physical violence or sexual assault during their lifetime."

Browne, Miller & Maguin, *Prevalence and Severity of Lifetime Physical and Sexual Victimization Among Incarcerated Women,* International Journal of Law & Psychiatry 22 (3-4) (1999).

Chapter 8: Faith Behind Bars
[8] "Religion defines evil and gives people the moral strength to resist."

Philip Yancey, *What's So Amazing About Grace?* Zondervan, 1997, p. 137.

Chapter 9: Let's Shout To The Lord
[9] "The Gospel is better news in prison than anywhere else because these people really understand the depths of their own sin." Charles Colson

Peggy Wehmeyer. *American Agenda—Religion in Prisons,* ABC News, December 20, 1994 (Transcript # 4252-7).

[10] "Give Him Everything," Beki Hemmingway Kerkman, *Davey & Goliath*, Augsburg Fortress Press, 2002.

Chapter 10: Jailhouse Ingenuity
[11] "Nearly half (44%) of women in state prisons in 1998 had not completed high school."

Lawrence A. Greenfeld and Tracy L. Snell, Women Offenders, Bureau of Justice Statistics 1997.

Chapter 11: P.O. Box 666
[12] "To imprison a woman is to remove her voice from the world, but many female inmates have been silenced by life long before the transport van carries them from the courthouse to the correctional facility."

Lamb, Wally, *Couldn't Keep It to Myself, Testimonies from our Imprisoned Sisters,* Regan Books, 2003, p.9.

Chapter 12: Robyn
[13] "Drug and Alcohol abuse play a role in the incarceration of 80% of the individuals imprisoned in U.S. jails and prisons."

National Center on Addiction and Substance Abuse at Columbia University, January 1998.

Chapter 13: Gooch
[14] "Nationwide, more than 57% of women in state prisons and 55% of women in local jails report having been physically and/or sexually abused in the past."

Prior Abuse Reported by Inmates and Probationers, Bureau of Justice Statistics, April 1999.

Chapter 14: Pamela

[15] "One of the most striking characteristics of incarcerated women is that the proportion who are of racial and ethnic minority background greatly exceeds their representation in the general population."

Amnesty USA, *Not Part of My Sentence, Violation of the Human Rights of Women in Custody,* p.1.

Chapter 15: Diane

[16] "Nearly one in three women in state prisons reported committing their offense to support a drug addiction."

William J. Sabol, Todd D. Minton and Paige Harrison, *Prison and Jail Inmates at Midyear 2006,* Bureau of Justice Statistics, U.S. Department of Justice.

Chapter 16: Tammie

[17] "If all inmates who needed treatment and aftercare received such services, the nation would break even in a year if just over 10 percent remained substance-and crime-free and employed."

Behind Bars II: Substance Abuse and America's Prison Population, The National Center on Addiction and Substance Abuse (CASA) at Columbia University.

Chapter 17: Michelle

[18] "After parental incarceration, a child whose father is imprisoned usually lives with the mother, while the child of an incarcerated mother is much more likely to live with grandparents, other relatives, or to be placed with foster care agencies."

Bloom, Barbara, David Steinhart, *Why Punish the Children? A Reappraisal of the Children of Incarcerated Mothers in America,* San Francisco, California: National Council on Crime and Delinquency, 1993.

Acoca, Leslie and Myrna S. Raeder, *Severing Family Ties: The Plight of Nonviolent Female Offenders and Their Children,* Stanford Law Policy Review, 11(1):133-151, 1999.

National Council on Crime and Delinquency, "The Plight of Children Whose Parents Are in Prison."

Chapter 18: Star

[19] "Over three million children witness domestic violence each year."

Mary Kenning, Anita Merchant and Alan Tomkins, *Research on the Effects of Witnessing Parental Battering: Clinical and Legal Policy Implications, in Women Battering:* Policy Implications, ed. Michael Steinman, (Cincinnati: Anderson Publishers, 1991).

Women In Prison Project, Correctional Association of New York, March 2002.

Chapter 19: Lynn

[20] "Studies also show that girls who have been sexually abused are more likely to be arrested as adults for prostitution."

C. Spatz–Widom and M.A. Ames, *"Criminal Consequences of Childhood Sexual Victimization,"* Child Abuse and Neglect, 18, 303-318 (1994).

Chapter 20: Yolanda

[21] "In its various shapes and sizes, female criminality is based on the need for women, excluded from conventional institutions, to survive under conditions not of their own making."

Chesney-Lind, 1997. *The Female Offender: Girls, Women, and Crime.* Thousand Oaks, CA: Sage Publications. Owen, Barbara, 1998 *"In the Mix: Struggle and Survival in a Women's Prison*, Albany, NY: SUNY Press.

Chapter 21: Ann

[22] "The story of women in prison reflects their status in society—a status that reflects ingrained racism and sexism, the subtle de-valuation of women and girls, and the open toleration of sexual and domestic abuse in a male-dominated society."

Barbara Owen, *Women in Prison*, California State University Press, 2008.

Chapter 22: Tesa

[23] "More than half of all prison and jail inmates have mental health problems."

Bureau of Justice Statistics, 2006.

Part Three: A Brief Guide To Jail and Prison Ministry

[24] "The historic role of the church combined with its potential for volunteer resources uniquely position the faith community to support the successful reintegration of returning prisoners."

Department of Health and Human Services, USA

—∿—

DISCUSSION QUESTIONS

1. What did you find surprising about the statistics introduced in this book?

2. How are those statistics reflected in the stories written by the women in Part Two?

3. What factors influence our beliefs about people who go to jail and prison?

4. Did your opinion of women offenders change as you read the book?

5. All of us make daily choices that have moral implications. How do the circumstances of our lives impact those choices?

6. In what ways are the stories uplifting despite the sadness in the women's lives?

7. How do you think suffering affects an individual's faith?

8. What life lessons can be learned from the women of Block 12?

9. Do you think there are solutions to the problem of recidivism?

10. Can one person or a group of people, really make a difference?

11. In Matthew 25, Jesus talks about visiting him in prison. What does that mean to you personally?

12. Did the book change your life in a positve or negative way?